Ninja Dual Zone Air Fryer Cookbook UK

Super-Simple Air Fryer Recipes to Help You Get Started with
Ninja Foodi MAX Dual Zone Air Fryer

Cherise Breslin

© Copyright 2023 – All Rights Reserved

The content contained within this book may not be reproduced, duplicated or transmitted without direct written permission from the author or the publisher.

Under no circumstances will any blame or legal responsibility be held against the publisher, or author, for any damages, reparation, or monetary loss due to the information contained within this book, either directly or indirectly.

▶ **Legal Notice:**

This book is copyright protected. It is only for personal use. You cannot amend, distribute, sell, use, quote or paraphrase any part, or the content within this book, without the consent of the author or publisher.

▶ **Disclaimer Notice:**

Please note the information contained within this document is for educational and entertainment purposes only. All effort has been executed to present accurate, up to date, reliable, complete information. No warranties of any kind are declared or implied. Readers acknowledge that the author is not engaged in the rendering of legal, financial, medical or professional advice. The content within this book has been derived from various sources. Please consult a licensed professional before attempting any techniques outlined in this book.

By reading this document, the reader agrees that under no circumstances is the author responsible for any losses, direct or indirect, that are incurred as a result of the use of the information contained within this document, including, but not limited to, errors, omissions, or inaccuracies.

Contents

1   Introduction

2   Fundamentals of Ninja Foodi 2-Basket Air Fryer

Important Safeguards 2
Getting to Know Your Ninja Foodi 2 Basket Air Fryer 2
Benefits of Ninja Foodi 2-Basket Air Fryer 3
Before First Use 4
Cooking in Your Ninja Foodi 2 Basket Air Fryer 4
Cleaning Your Ninja 2-Basket Air Fryer 8
Helpful Tips 8
Replacement Parts 8
Troubleshooting Guide 9
Warranty 9

10   4-Week Meal Plan

Week 1 10   Week 3 11
Week 2 10   Week 4 11

12   Chapter 1 Breakfast

Stuffed Mushrooms 12   Turkey with Cheese and Pasilla
Cheese Cauliflower Balls 13   Peppers 15
Greek Feta Frittata 14   Greek Omelet with Cheese 15
Crispy Cheese Spinach Balls 14   Sausage Omelet 16

Manchego & Cauliflower Patties	16	Tasty Gruyère Stuffed Mushrooms	20
Eggs with Beef and Tomato	17	Chicken Sausage Frittata	20
Broccoli Fritters	17	Cheese Asparagus Casserole	21
Cheese Mushroom Balls	18	Chili Cauliflower Florets	22
Celery & Bacon Croquettes	19	Cauliflower and Broccoli	22
Smoked Tofu Omelet	19		

22 Chapter 2 Vegetables and Sides

Courgette Noodles	23	Unseasoned Beetroot	28
Coated Jicama Sticks	23	Panko Broccoli Tots	28
Spiced Broccoli Steaks	24	Simple Brussels Sprouts	29
Easy Aubergine Slices	24	Lemon Pepper-Seasoned Cauliflower	29
Turmeric Cauliflower Steaks	25	Potato Pot with Sauce	30
Garlicky Courgette Slices	25	Corn Croquettes	31
Kale in Beef Stock	26	Fresh Corn on the Cob	31
Trimmed Asparagus	26	Creole Gold Potato Wedges	32
Crispy Asparagus Fries	27	Vinegar-Seasoned Chicken Wings	33
Green Beans with Ground Coriander	27	Easy-to-Make Duck Skin	33

33 Chapter 3 Poultry

Coconut Chicken Breast	34	Thanksgiving Turkey	40
Mustard Marinated Chicken	34	Loaded Turkey Meatloaf	41
Sweet-Sour Chicken Drumsticks	35	Tangy Chicken with Parsley	41
Skinless Chicken Thighs	35	Chicken with Smoked Bacon	42
Tarragon-Seasoned Chicken Thighs	36	Turkey Thighs with Vegetables	43
Nutty Turkey Breast	36	Chicken with Leeks	44
Eggs & Sausage Keto Rolls	37	Chicken Sliders in Chili Sauce	44
Bacon-Wrapped Turkey	38	Italian-Style Chicken Breasts	45
Typical Chicken Nuggets	38	Rustic Turkey Breasts	46
Aromatic Turkey Breast	39	T-Bone Steak with Aromatics	47
Pepper Chicken Cutlets	39		

Chapter 4 Beef, Pork, and Lamb — 47

Tangy Beef Strips 48	Spicy Steak Pieces 55
Lemony Beef Steaks 49	Filet Mignon with Peanut Sauce ... 56
Beef Chops with Coriander........ 50	Rich Meatloaf 57
Beef Chops with Salad 51	Spicy Steak 58
Beef with Pearl Onions and Cauliflower 52	Beef Tenderloins in Beef Stock ... 58
	Meatballs with Spicy Sauce 59
Teriyaki Steak 53	Filet Mignon Steaks 60
Beef Bulgogi Burgers 54	Whisky Steak 61
Beer-Braised Beef 54	Beef Cubes with Aubergine 61
Asian Steak Strips 55	Lemon Cod Fillets 62

Chapter 5 Fish and Seafood — 62

Cauliflower & White Fish Cakes 63	Lemony Prawns 70
Sea Scallops in Beer 64	Tilapia with Caper Sauce 71
Crusted Flounder Fillets 64	Flounder with Chives 72
Fish Gratin 65	Crab & Cauliflower Cakes 73
Coconut Tilapia 66	Salmon with Coriander Sauce...... 73
French Sea Bass 66	Rockfish Fillets with Avocado Cream 74
Sole Fish and Cauliflower Fritters 67	Cod Fillets with Lemon 75
Salmon Burgers 68	Crab Cakes with Capers 76
Crusted Tilapia Fillets.............. 69	Banana Peppers with Cheese 77
Garlicky Prawns 69	Parmesan Cauliflower.............. 77
Salmon Steaks with Butter and Wine 70	

Chapter 6 Snacks and Starters — 77

Keto Coleslaw....................... 78	Cream Cauliflower 80
Coconut Brussels Sprouts 78	Cheese Asparagus 81
Mustard Cabbage Steaks........... 79	Cauliflower and Asparagus 81
Cheese Tomatillos Slices 79	Yummy Chicken Bites 82
Turnip Bites......................... 80	Courgette Slices with Mozzarella

Cheese 82	Courgette Crackers 84
Cheese Kale Chips 83	Olives Cakes 85
Mozzarella Portobello Pizza 83	Cheddar Pork Minis 85
Easy Parmesan Chips 84	Chocolate Raspberry Cake 86

86 — Chapter 7 Desserts

White Chocolate Cookies 87	Blackberry Muffins 92
Puffy Pecan Cookies 88	Cookies with Chocolate Chips ... 93
Flourless Almond Cookies 89	Keto Berry Crumble Pots 94
Walnuts Tart 89	Vanilla Chocolate Cake 95
Old-Fashioned Raspberries Muffins 90	Chocolate Fudge Cake 96
Double Chocolate Brownies 91	Puffy Coconut Cookies 97

98 — Conclusion

99 — Appendix Recipes Index

Introduction

If you're looking for a versatile appliance that can do it all, the Ninja Foodi 2 Basket Air Fryer is a great option. This appliance can air fry, bake, roast, and dehydrate, all in one. And with two baskets, you can cook multiple items at once. The Ninja Foodi 2 Basket Air Fryer is a versatile and convenient appliance that can help you with all of your cooking needs. With two baskets, you can cook multiple items at once, making it a great option for large families or those who entertain often. This appliance can air fry, bake, roast, and dehydrate, so you can make a variety of recipes. And with a variety of accessories available, you can customize your Cooking experience. This is a great feature for those who want to be able to cook multiple items at the same time. The Ninja Foodi 2 Basket Air Fryer is also a great choice for those who want to be able to cook a variety of foods. The Ninja Foodi 2 Basket Air Fryer is a great choice for those who want to be able to cook multiple items at the same time.

Fundamentals of Ninja Foodi 2-Basket Air Fryer

Important Safeguards

If you're like most people, you probably think of an air fryer as a healthier way to cook French fries and other fried foods. And while that's true, there's so much more than an air fryer can do! Ninja 2-Basket Air Fryer is a versatile appliance that can be used for a variety of tasks, from roasting and baking to dehydrating and even air frying. But as with any appliance, certain safety precautions should be followed when using an air fryer. Here are a few important safeguards to keep in mind:

When using your Ninja® 2-Basket Air Fryer, it is important to take some basic safety precautions to help prevent injuries and damage to your appliance. Here are some important things to keep in mind:

Always use the Ninja® 2-Basket Air Fryer on a level, stable surface.

Never leave the Ninja® 2-Basket Air Fryer unattended while it is in use.

Be sure to unplug the Ninja® 2-Basket Air Fryer from the power outlet when not in use and before cleaning.

Do not use the Ninja® 2-Basket Air Fryer if it is damaged in any way. If the appliance is damaged, stop using it immediately and contact Ninja® customer service for assistance.

To help prevent the risk of electric shock, do not immerse the appliance in water or other liquids.

Keep your hands and fingers away from the hot air fryer basket and heating element.

Never place anything other than food in the air fryer

Getting to Know Your Ninja Foodi 2 Basket Air Fryer

If you are looking for a healthier way to fry your food, then you may want to consider the Ninja 2 Basket Air Fryer. This unique appliance uses little to no oil to fry your food, making it a healthier alternative to traditional deep frying. So how does it work? The Ninja 2 Basket Air Fryer uses super-heated air to cook your food. This hot air circulates the food, cooking it evenly and quickly. And because there is no oil involved, you don't have to worry about your food being greasy or unhealthy. If you're looking for a versatile air fryer that can do it all, the Ninja® Foodi™ 5-in-1 Indoor Grill with 4-Quart Air Fryer is the perfect appliance for your kitchen. This grill can air fry, bake, roast, and dehydrate all in one appliance, making it a true powerhouse in the kitchen. And with the Ninja Air Crisp® Technology, you can enjoy perfectly cooked food with a crispy, golden exterior and a juicy, tender interior.

Operating Buttons

1 Controls the output for the basket on the left.

2 Controls the output for the basket on the right.

TEMP arrows: Use the up and down arrows to adjust the cook temperature before or during cooking.

TIME arrows: Use the up and down arrows to adjust the cook time in any function before or during the cook cycle.

SMART FINISH button: Automatically syncs the cook times to ensure both zones finish at the same time, even if there are different cook times.

MATCH COOK button: Automatically matches zone 2 settings to those of zone 1 to cook a larger amount of the same food, or cook different foods using the same function, temperature, and time.

START/PAUSE button: After selecting temperature and time, start cooking by pressing the START/PAUSE button. To pause cooking, first select the zone you would like to pause, then press the START/PAUSE button.

POWER button: The button turns the unit on and off and stops all cooking functions. Standby Mode: After 10 minutes of no interaction with the control panel, the unit will enter standby mode. The Power button will be dimly lit. Hold Mode: Hold will appear on the unit while in SMART FINISH mode. One zone will be cooking, while the other zone will be holding until the times sync together.

Functions Buttons

Air Broil: Add the crispy finishing touch to meals, or melt toppings to create the perfect finish.

Air Fry: Use this function to give your food crispiness and crunch with little to no oil.

Roast: Use the unit as a roaster oven for tender meats and more.

Reheat: Warm your leftovers, with a crispy result.

Dehydrate: Dehydrate meats, fruits, and vegetables for healthy snacks.

Bake: Create decadent baked treats and desserts.

Benefits of Ninja Foodi 2-Basket Air Fryer

The Ninja 2 Basket Air Fryer is a top-of-the-line air fryer with multiple functions to make your cooking experience better than ever. One of the best features of the Ninja 2 Basket Air Fryer is the multiple operating buttons that make it so user-friendly. Here is a run-down of all the different operating buttons on the Ninja 2 Basket Air Fryer and what each one does: There are many different types of air fryers on the market, but the Ninja 2 Basket Air Fryer is one of the best. This air fryer has two baskets that can be used to cook food at the same time. The Ninja® Air Fryer 2 Basket System is the first of its kind. This revolutionary kitchen appliance gives you the power to cook two foods at once with little to no oil. The secret is the innovative dual-layer racks that allow hot air to circulate evenly around both food items for perfectly cooked results every time. The Ninja 2 Basket Air Fryer also has several different settings that can be used to cook food to perfection.

The Ninja Air Fryer 2 Basket System comes with a variety of features that make it easy to use, including:
- AnLCDy that clearly shows the cooking time and temperature
- A detachable cooking pot that is easy to clean
- A variety of pre-set cooking functions for common foods
- A safety shut-off feature that prevents the appliance from overheating
- A cool-touch exterior that stays safe to the touch even when the appliance is in use
- An easily removable drip tray that catches any excess oil or grease
- Dishwasher-safe parts for easy cleanup

Before First Use

Before first use of the Ninja® 2 Basket Air Fryer, be sure to read all instructions in the Owner's Guide. Wash the removable parts in warm, soapy water and dry them thoroughly. Do not use any harsh cleaners or abrasives. Season the cookware by spraying with cooking spray and heating on the Air Fryer base for 3 minutes. It is always exciting to get a new appliance, and an air fryer is a great addition to any kitchen. But before you can start cooking with your new air fryer, there are a few things you need to do first. Here is a quick guide on how to prepare your Ninja 2-Basket Air Fryer before its first use.

Remove all of the packaging materials from the air fryer. This includes the user manual, warranty information, and any other literature that came with the unit.

Wash the air fryer baskets in warm, soapy water. Rinse them well and dry them completely before using them.

Season the air fryer baskets with cooking oil. This will help to prevent food from sticking to the baskets and ensure even cooking.

Preheat the air fryer to the desired cooking temperature. Refer to the user manual for guidance on how to do this.

Cooking in Your Ninja Foodi 2 Basket Air Fryer

If you love the taste of fried foods but don't want all the oil and mess that comes with traditional frying, then you'll love cooking in your Ninja Foodi 2 Basket Air Fryer. This incredible appliance can do it all, and it's so easy to use. With the Ninja Foodi 2 Basket Air Fryer, you can cook multiple items at once, so it's great for feeding a crowd. Plus, there's no need to preheat the air fryer, so you can save even more time. And clean-up is dual-zone thanks to the removable, dishwasher-safe baskets. So what can you cook in your Ninja Foodi 2 Basket Air Fryer? Just about anything! Chicken, fish, beef, pork, vegetables, French fries, and even desserts can all be cooked to perfection in the air fryer.

Cooking with Dual-Zone Technology

This type of air fryer allows you to cook two different types of food at the same time. This is perfect for those who want to try new recipes or for those who want to cook a variety of food at the same time. One of the best things about dual zone air fryers is that they come with two baskets. This means that you can cook two different types of food at the same time. This is perfect for those who want to try new recipes or for those who want to cook a variety of food at the same time. Another great thing about dual zone air fryers is they have a timer. This means that you can set the timer for each basket. This is perfect for those who want to cook a variety of food at the same time. This amazing kitchen appliance can help you cook two meals at once, or even cook a large meal for a family. With two independent cooking zones, you can cook different foods at different temperatures, so you can cook a variety of foods at once. The Ninja 2 Basket Air Fryer also features a dehydrator function, so you can dehydrate foods like fruits and vegetables for snacks or for use in recipes.

Pausing and Ending Cook Times

When it comes to your Ninja 2 Basket Air Fryer, there may come a time when you need to pause or end your cooking cycle. Whether you need to step away for a moment or your food is done cooking, it's important to know how to properly pause or end your cooking cycle. Here's a quick guide on how to do just that: If you need to step away from your Ninja 2 Basket Air Fryer for a moment, simply press the "Pause" button on the control panel. This will pause your cooking cycle and keep your food warm until you're ready to resume cooking. To resume cooking, simply press the "Start" button. If your food is done cooking, press the "Stop" button on the control panel to end your cooking cycle and your food will remain warm until you're ready to serve.

Pausing Time in a Single Zone

When you think of an air fryer, you probably think of fried chicken or French fries. But did you know that you can also use an air fryer to pause time? That's right, with the power of hot air, you can pause time in a single zoon in an air fryer. Just set the timer for the desired amount of time and let the air fryers do their magic. Now, you might be thinking, why would I want to pause time? Well, there are actually quite a few reasons. For one, it can be a great dual-zone ok food evenly. By pausing time, dual-zone to make sure that all sides of your food are cooked evenly. Another on to pause time is to prevent overcooking. If you're worried about your food getting overcooked, pausing time can help to prevent that. Finally, pausing time can also cook time as a way to keep food warm.

Ending the Cook Time in One Zone (While Using Both Zone)

Air fryers are cook-time devices that can cook food quickly and evenly. However, sometimes you may want to cook two things at once. This is where the dual zone air fryer comes in handy! With a dual-zone fryer, you can cook two items at once, with each item in its own cooking zone. This means that you can cook two items at different temperatures, so that one is perfectly cooked while the other is still cooking. If you want to end cook time in 1 zoon, simply set the timer for the desired cook time and wait for the food to be done. Once the cooking time is up, the air fryer will automatically turn off, so you don't have to worry about overcooking your food.

Cooking in a Single Zone

When it comes to cooking for one, the Ninja® 2-Basket Air Fryer is the perfect tool. It's large enough to cook a meal for one, but small enough to fit on a countertop. Plus, it comes with two baskets, so you can cook multiple items at the same time. Air frying is a great way to cook for one because it's quick and easy. Plus, you can cook a variety of foods in the air fryer, from chicken and fish to veggies and French fries. And, since the air fryer uses little to no oil, it's a healthier option than traditional frying methods. Air frying is a process of cooking food in an air fryer. Ninja Foodi 2-Basket Air Fryer is a great appliance for air frying. It is a two-basket air fryer that can accommodate two servings of food at a time. The Ninja Foodi 2-Basket Air Fryer is a great choice for those who want to cook their food in an air fryer but don't want to spend a lot of money on an air fryer. The Ninja Foodi 2-Basket Air Fryer is a great appliance for those who want to cook their food in an air fryer but don't want to spend a lot of money on an air fryer.

Air Fry:

When it comes to air frying, the Ninja Foodi 2 Basket Air Fryer is a powerhouse. It can handle large batches of food with ease, and it produces crispy, evenly-cooked food every time. If you're looking for a versatile air fryer that can handle anything you throw at it, the Ninja Foodi 2 Basket Air Fryer is the one for you. When it comes to cooking times, the Ninja Foodi 2 Basket Air Fryer is pretty fast. It can cook a large batch of food in as little as 20 minutes, so you won't have to wait long for your food to be ready. And, because it uses air fryer technology, your food will be cooked evenly and crisply, without the need for any oil. So, if you're looking for an air fryer that can handle large batches of food and produces perfectly cooked results every time, the Ninja Foodi 2 Basket Air Fryer is the one for you.

Bake:

One of the great things about the Ninja Foodi 2 Basket Air Fryer is that it can do so much more than just fry food. It can also bake, and it does a great job at it! baking in the Ninja Foodi 2 Basket Air Fryer is a breeze, and it produces great results. The key to success is to use the right settings and to preheat the unit before you start baking. Here are a few tips for baking in the Ninja Foodi 2 Basket Air Fryer:

- Preheat the unit before you start baking. This will help ensure that your food cooks evenly.
- Use the bake setting on the Ninja Foodi 2 Basket Air Fryer.
- Make sure that you use an oven-safe baking dish or pan.
- Follow the recipe directions closely.
- Check your food periodically to ensure it is cooking properly.

Roast:

Air frying is a healthier alternative to deep frying because it uses less oil. The Ninja Foodi 2 Basket Air Fryer is a great appliance for air frying because it has two baskets that can be used at the same time. This means that you can cook multi-plant in a healthier way. Air frying is a simple process that involves using hot air to cook food. The food is placed in a basket and the basket is placed in the air fryer. The air fryer circulates hot air around the food, cooking it evenly. One of the great things about air frying is that it can be used to cook a variety of foods. Chicken, fish, vegetables, and even desserts can be cooked in an air fryer. And because air frying uses less oil, it is a healthier option than deep frying. If you are looking for a healthier way to cook, then consider air frying.

Reheat:

When it comes to reheating food, the Ninja Foodi 2 Basket Air Fryer is a powerhouse. It can reheat food quickly and evenly, thanks to its powerful air fryer function. Plus, it has a built-in reheat function that makes it easy to reheat your food without having to guess at cook times or temperatures. Here are a few tips for reheating food in your Ninja Foodi 2 Basket Air Fryer:

- Preheat the air fryer to the desired reheat temperature before adding your food.
- If you're reheating multiple items, space them out evenly in the baskets so that they reheat evenly.
- Reheat food in batches if necessary, depending on how much food you're reheating at once.
- Use the air fryer's built-in reheat function for the best results. Simply select the reheat function and then choose the desired temperature and time.

Dehydrate:

Dehydrating in the Ninja Foodi 2 Basket Air Fryer is a great way to preserve food. This method of drying food removes the water content, leaving behind the nutrients and flavor. Dehydration protects food from spoilage and makes it easier to store and transport. To dehydrate in the Ninja Foodi 2 Basket Air Fryer, simply place the food in the basket and set the temperature to 165 degrees Fahrenheit. The drying process will take several hours, depending on the type and thickness of the food. Check the food periodically to make sure it is drying evenly. Once the food is dried, it can be stored in an airtight container in the refrigerator for up to six months. Dehydrated food is a great way to have healthy, nutritious snacks on hand at all times.

Air Broil:

Air Broiling in the Ninja Foodi 2 Basket Air Fryer is a great way to cook food. The air fryer cooks food by circulating hot air around it, so it cooks evenly and quickly. This is a great way to cook chicken, fish, or vegetables. Air broiling is also a great way to cook food that is normally difficult to cook, such as burgers or steak.

Cleaning Your Ninja 2-Basket Air Fryer

Cleaning your Ninja 2-Basket Air Fryer is pretty simple and doesn't take too much time. First, you'll want to unplug the air fryer and remove any food or debris from the baskets. Next, you'll want to wash the baskets in warm, soapy water. Once they're clean, you can dry them off and put them back in the air fryer. To clean the exterior of the air fryer, you can use a damp cloth or paper towel to wipe down the outside. If there are any tough stains, you can use a mild cleaning solution. Be sure to avoid any harsh chemicals or abrasive cleaners, as they could damage the finish. Once you've cleaned the outside and the baskets, you can plug the air fryer back in and get ready to cook up some delicious food!

Helpful Tips

If you're one of the many people who have recently purchased a Ninja 2-Basket Air Fryer, you may be wondering how to get the most out of your new appliance. Here are a few helpful tips for making delicious air fryer recipes:

- Preheat your air fryer before adding any ingredients. This will help ensure that your food cooks evenly.
- Cut your ingredients into uniform pieces. This will also help with even cooking.
- Use an oil sprayer to coat your ingredients with oil. This will help them crisp up nicely in the air fryer.
- Don't overcrowd the air fryer baskets. Make sure there's plenty of space around each piece of food so that hot air can circulate properly.
- Flip your ingredients halfway through cooking. This will help them cook evenly on all sides.
- When in doubt, consult your air fryer's manual

Replacement Parts

If you're like most people, your Ninja 2-Basket Air Fryer is one of your favorite kitchen appliances. But like all appliances, it will eventually need some replacement parts. Here are some of the most common parts that need to be replaced on a Ninja 2-Basket Air Fryer:

1.The basket is the most important part of the air fryer and it's also the most likely to need replacing. Over time, the basket can become warped or damaged, making it difficult to cook food evenly. If you notice that your basket isn't cooking food as well as it used to, it's time for a replacement.

2. The Heating Element: The heating element is what helps the air fryer cook food quickly and evenly. Over time, the heating element can become damaged or burned out, making it less effective. If your air fryer isn't cooking food as well as it used to, it's probably time to replace the heating element.

Troubleshooting Guide

If you're having trouble with your Ninja 2-Basket Air Fryer, here's a troubleshooting guide to help you get back to frying up your favorite food. First, check to make sure that the air fryer is plugged in and that the power switch is turned on. If the air fryer still doesn't turn on, then it may be a problem with the power cord or the outlet. Next, check to see if the air fryer baskets are properly in place. If they're not, the air fryer won't be able to operate properly. If the baskets seem to be in place but the air fryer still isn't working, then there may be something blocking the airflow. Check the air fryer's vents to make sure they're not blocked by food or other debris. If the air fryer still isn't working after you've checked all of these things, there may bee's a problem with your air fryer. It's better to check the time with a professional checker.

Warranty

The Ninja Foodi 2-Basket Air Fryer is covered by a one-year limited warranty. This means that, if something goes wrong with your air fryer, you can contact Ninja customer service within one year of purchase to get it replaced or repaired. Of course, there are some limits to this warranty. It does not cover damages caused by accident, misuse, or abuse. So, if you drop your air fryer and it breaks, you won't be covered. Also, the warranty only applies to the original purchaser. If you buy a used Ninja Foodi 2-Basket Air Fryer, the warranty won't be valid. Overall, the Ninja Foodi 2-Basket Air Fryer is a great appliance with a solid warranty. If you take good care of it, you shouldn't have any problems. But if something does go wrong, you can rest assured that Ninja will take care of you.

4-Week Meal Plan

Week 1

Day 1:
Breakfast: Greek Feta Frittata
Lunch: Chili Cauliflower Florets
Snack: Banana Peppers with Cheese
Dinner: Vinegar-Seasoned Chicken Wings
Dessert: White Chocolate Cookies

Day 2:
Breakfast: Cheese Cauliflower Balls
Lunch: Coated Jicama Sticks
Snack: Parmesan Cauliflower
Dinner: Easy-to-Make Duck Skin
Dessert: Chocolate Raspberry Cake

Day 3:
Breakfast: Stuffed Mushrooms
Lunch: Cauliflower and Broccoli
Snack: Keto Coleslaw
Dinner: Tangy Beef Strips
Dessert: Puffy Pecan Cookies

Day 4:
Breakfast: Turkey with Cheese and Pasilla Peppers
Lunch: Courgette Noodles
Snack: Coconut Brussels Sprouts
Dinner: Lemon Cod Fillets
Dessert: Double Chocolate Brownies

Day 5:
Breakfast: Sausage Omelet
Lunch: Spiced Broccoli Steaks
Snack: Mustard Cabbage Steaks
Dinner: Coconut Chicken Breast
Dessert: Flourless Almond Cookies

Day 6:
Breakfast: Eggs with Beef and Tomato
Lunch: Easy Aubergine Slices
Snack: Cheese Tomatillos Slices
Dinner: T-Bone Steak with Aromatics
Dessert: Old-Fashioned Raspberries Muffins

Day 7:
Breakfast: Crispy Cheese Spinach Balls
Lunch: Turmeric Cauliflower Steaks
Snack: Turnip Bites
Dinner: Coconut Tilapia
Dessert: Blackberry Muffins

Week 2

Day 1:
Breakfast: Cheese Mushroom Balls
Lunch: Garlicky Courgette Slices
Snack: Cream Cauliflower
Dinner: Pepper Chicken Cutlets
Dessert: Walnuts Tart

Day 2:
Breakfast: Greek Omelet with Cheese
Lunch: Kale in Beef Stock
Snack: Cheese Asparagus
Dinner: Lemony Beef Steaks
Dessert: Cookies with Chocolate Chips

Day 3:
Breakfast: Broccoli Fritters
Lunch: Green Beans with Ground Coriander
Snack: Yummy Chicken Bites
Dinner: French Sea Bass
Dessert: Keto Berry Crumble Pots

Day 4:
Breakfast: Celery & Bacon Croquettes
Lunch: Trimmed Asparagus
Snack: Cauliflower and Asparagus
Dinner: Beef Chops with Coriander
Dessert: Vanilla Chocolate Cake

Day 5:
Breakfast: Smoked Tofu Omelet
Lunch: Crispy Asparagus Fries
Snack: Courgette Slices with Mozzarella Cheese
Dinner: Sweet-Sour Chicken Drumsticks
Dessert: Chocolate Fudge Cake

Day 6:
Breakfast: Manchego & Cauliflower Patties
Lunch: Unseasoned Beetroot
Snack: Cheese Kale Chips
Dinner: Nutty Turkey Breast
Dessert: Puffy Coconut Cookies

Day 7:
Breakfast: Tasty Gruyère Stuffed Mushrooms
Lunch: Panko Broccoli Tots
Snack: Mozzarella Portobello Pizza
Dinner: Beef with Pearl Onions and Cauliflower
Dessert: White Chocolate Cookies

Week 3

Day 1:
Breakfast: Cheese Asparagus Casserole
Lunch: Simple Brussels Sprouts
Snack: Easy Parmesan Chips
Dinner: Salmon Steaks with Butter and Wine
Dessert: Chocolate Raspberry Cake

Day 2:
Breakfast: Chicken Sausage Frittata
Lunch: Lemon Pepper-Seasoned Cauliflower
Snack: Courgette Crackers
Dinner: Tarragon-Seasoned Chicken Thighs
Dessert: Puffy Pecan Cookies

Day 3:
Breakfast: Stuffed Mushrooms
Lunch: Potato Pot with Sauce
Snack: Olives Cakes
Dinner: Bacon-Wrapped Turkey
Dessert: Old-Fashioned Raspberries Muffins

Day 4:
Breakfast: Greek Feta Frittata
Lunch: Corn Croquettes
Snack: Cheddar Pork Minis
Dinner: Beef Cubes with Aubergine
Dessert: Flourless Almond Cookies

Day 5:
Breakfast: Cheese Cauliflower Balls
Lunch: Fresh Corn on the Cob
Snack: Banana Peppers with Cheese
Dinner: Garlicky Prawns
Dessert: Double Chocolate Brownies

Day 6:
Breakfast: Turkey with Cheese and Pasilla Peppers
Lunch: Creole Gold Potato Wedges
Snack: Parmesan Cauliflower
Dinner: Italian-Style Chicken Breasts
Dessert: Blackberry Muffins

Day 7:
Breakfast: Sausage Omelet
Lunch: Chili Cauliflower Florets
Snack: Keto Coleslaw
Dinner: Spicy Steak
Dessert: Walnuts Tart

Week 4

Day 1:
Breakfast: Eggs with Beef and Tomato
Lunch: Coated Jicama Sticks
Snack: Coconut Brussels Sprouts
Dinner: Tilapia with Caper Sauce
Dessert: Cookies with Chocolate Chips

Day 2:
Breakfast: Crispy Cheese Spinach Balls
Lunch: Cauliflower and Broccoli
Snack: Mustard Cabbage Steaks
Dinner: Turkey Thighs with Vegetables
Dessert: Keto Berry Crumble Pots

Day 3:
Breakfast: Greek Omelet with Cheese
Lunch: Courgette Noodles
Snack: Cheese Tomatillos Slices
Dinner: Typical Chicken Nuggets
Dessert: Vanilla Chocolate Cake

Day 4:
Breakfast: Cheese Mushroom Balls
Lunch: Spiced Broccoli Steaks
Snack: Turnip Bites
Dinner: Filet Mignon with Peanut Sauce
Dessert: Puffy Coconut Cookies

Day 5:
Breakfast: Broccoli Fritters
Lunch: Easy Aubergine Slices
Snack: Cheese Asparagus
Dinner: Cod Fillets with Lemon
Dessert: Chocolate Fudge Cake

Day 6:
Breakfast: Celery & Bacon Croquettes
Lunch: Turmeric Cauliflower Steaks
Snack: Yummy Chicken Bites
Dinner: Loaded Turkey Meatloaf
Dessert: White Chocolate Cookies

Day 7:
Breakfast: Smoked Tofu Omelet
Lunch: Garlicky Courgette Slices
Snack: Cheese Kale Chips
Dinner: Teriyaki Steak
Dessert: Chocolate Raspberry Cake

Chapter 1 Breakfast

Stuffed Mushrooms

Prep time: 15 minutes | Cook time: 15 minutes | Serves: 5

50g parmesan cheese, grated

2 cloves garlic, pressed

2 tablespoons fresh coriander, chopped

⅓ teaspoon salt

½ teaspoon crushed red pepper flakes

1½ tablespoons olive oil

20 medium-sized mushrooms cut off the stems

50g Gorgonzola cheese, grated

60g low-fat mayonnaise

1 teaspoon prepared horseradish, well-drained

1 tablespoon fresh parsley, finely chopped

1. Mix the parmesan cheese together with the garlic, coriander, salt, red pepper, and the olive oil. 2. Stuff the mushroom caps with the parmesan filling. Top them with grated Gorgonzola. 3. Insert the crisper plates in the baskets. Divide the stuffed mushrooms between the baskets in zone 1 and zone 2. 4. Select AIR FRY mode, adjust the cooking temperature to 190°C and set the cooking time to 12 minutes. 5. Press the MATCH COOK button and copy the zone 1 settings to zone 2. 6. Press the START/PAUSE button to begin cooking. 7. Mix the mayonnaise, horseradish and parsley to make the horseradish, and then serve with the warm fried mushrooms.

Cheese Cauliflower Balls

Prep time: 15 minutes | Cook time: 15 minutes | Serves: 4

100g cauliflower florets

120ml roasted vegetable stock

1 egg, beaten

100g white mushrooms, finely chopped

50g parmesan cheese, grated

3 garlic cloves, peeled and minced

½ yellow onion, finely chopped

⅓ teaspoon ground black pepper, or more to taste

1½ peppers, seeded minced

½ chipotle pepper, seeded and minced

50g cheese, grated

1½ tablespoons rapeseed oil

Sea salt, to savor

1. Blitz the cauliflower florets in your food processor until they're crumbled (it is the size of rice). 2. Heat the oil in a saucepan over medium heat; sweat the garlic, onions, pepper, cauliflower rice, and chipotle pepper until tender. 3. Throw in the mushrooms and fry them until they are fragrant and the liquid has almost evaporated. 4. Add in the stock and boil for 18 minutes. 5. Add the cheese and spices; mix to combine. 6. Turn off the heat and allow the mixture to cool completely. 7. Shape the mixture into balls. Dip the balls in the beaten egg; then, roll them over the grated parmesan. 8. Insert the crisper plate in the basket in zone 1, and transfer the balls to it. 9. Select AIR FRY mode, adjust the cooking temperature to 205°C and set the cooking time to 6 minutes. 10. Press the START/PAUSE button to begin cooking. 11. Serve with marinara sauce and enjoy!

Greek Feta Frittata

Prep time: 10 minutes | Cook time: 10 minutes | Serves: 4

60g Feta cheese, crumbled

1 teaspoon dried rosemary

2 tablespoons fish sauce

210g cooked chicken breasts, boneless and shredded

½ teaspoon coriander sprig, finely chopped

6 medium-sized whisked eggs

⅓ teaspoon ground white pepper

35g fresh chives, chopped

½ teaspoon garlic paste

Fine sea salt, to taste

Nonstick cooking spray

1. Combine all of the ingredients except for the cheese in a bowl. 2. Insert the crisper plate in the basket in zone 1, and transfer the mixture to it. 3. Select AIR FRY mode, adjust the cooking temperature to 180°C and set the cooking time to 8 minutes. 4. Press the START/PAUSE button to begin cooking. 5. Scatter crumbled feta over the top of the dish and eat immediately!

Crispy Cheese Spinach Balls

Prep time: 15 minutes | Cook time: 15 minutes | Serves: 4

60ml milk

2 eggs

100g cheese

60g spinach, torn into pieces

35g flaxseed meal

½ teaspoon baking powder

2 tablespoons rapeseed oil

Salt and ground black pepper, to taste

1. Add all the ingredients to a food processor or blender, and then puree the ingredients until it becomes dough. 2. Roll the dough into small balls. 3. Insert the crisper plates in the baskets. Divide the dough balls the baskets in zone 1 and zone 2. 4. Select AIR FRY mode, adjust the cooking temperature to 155°C and set the cooking time to 12 minutes. 5. Press the MATCH COOK button and copy the zone 1 settings to zone 2. 6. Press the START/PAUSE button to begin cooking. 7. Serve hot.

Turkey with Cheese and Pasilla Peppers

Prep time: 30 minutes | Cook time: 30 minutes | Serves: 2

50g Parmesan cheese, shredded

225g turkey breasts, cut into four pieces

80g mayonnaise

1½ tablespoons sour cream

1 dried Pasilla peppers

1 teaspoon onion salt

⅓ teaspoon mixed peppercorns, freshly cracked

1. In a shallow bowl, mix Parmesan cheese, onion salt, and the cracked mixed peppercorns together. 2. In a food processor, blitz the mayonnaise, along with the cream and dried Pasilla peppers until there are no lumps. 3. Coat the turkey breasts with this mixture, ensuring that all sides are covered. 4. Coat each piece of turkey in the Parmesan mixture. 5. Insert the crisper plates in the baskets. Divide the turkey pieces between the baskets in zone 1 and zone 2. 6. Select AIR FRY mode, adjust the cooking temperature to 185°C and set the cooking time to 28 minutes. 7. Press the MATCH COOK button and copy the zone 1 settings to zone 2. 8. Press the START/PAUSE button to begin cooking. 9. Serve hot.

Greek Omelet with Cheese

Prep time: 17 minutes | Cook time: 15 minutes | Serves: 2

65g Halloumi cheese, sliced

2 teaspoons garlic paste

2 teaspoons fresh chopped rosemary

4 well-whisked eggs

2 peppers, seeded and chopped

1½ tablespoons fresh basil, chopped

3 tablespoons onions, chopped

Fine sea salt and ground black pepper, to taste

1. Mix all of the ingredients in a large bowl until everything is well incorporated. 2. Transfer the mixture to the basket in zone 1. 3. Select AIR FRY mode, adjust the cooking temperature to 160°C and set the cooking time to 15 minutes. 4. Press the START/PAUSE button to begin cooking. 5. Serve warm.

Sausage Omelet

Prep time: 15 minutes | Cook time: 10 minutes | Serves: 5

3 pork sausages, chopped

8 well-beaten eggs

1½ peppers, seeded and chopped

1 teaspoon smoked cayenne pepper

2 tablespoons shredded cheese

½ teaspoon tarragon

½ teaspoon ground black pepper

1 teaspoon salt

1. In a cast-iron frying pan, sweat the peppers together with the chopped pork sausages until the peppers are fragrant and the sausage begins to release liquid. 2. Insert the crisper plates in the baskets. 3. Divide the sausage mixture and all of the remaining ingredients between the baskets in zone 1 and zone 2. 4. Select BAKE mode, adjust the cooking temperature to 175°C and set the cooking time to 9 minutes. 5. Press the MATCH COOK button and copy the zone 1 settings to zone 2. 6. Press the START/PAUSE button to begin cooking. 7. Serve right away with the salad of your choice.

Manchego & Cauliflower Patties

Prep time: 15 minutes | Cook time: 10 minutes | Serves: 4

100g Manchego cheese, shredded

1 teaspoon paprika

1 teaspoon freshly ground black pepper

½ tablespoon fine sea salt

80g spring onions, finely chopped

455g cauliflower florets

2 tablespoons rapeseed oil

2 teaspoons dried basil

1. Blitz the cauliflower florets in a food processor until finely crumbed. Combine the broccoli with the rest of the above ingredients. 2. Shape the balls using your hands. Flatten the balls to make the patties. 3. Insert the crisper plates in the baskets. Divide the patties between the baskets in zone 1 and zone 2. 4. Select AIR FRY mode, adjust the cooking temperature to 180°C and set the cooking time to 10 minutes. 5. Press the MATCH COOK button and copy the zone 1 settings to zone 2. 6. Press the START/PAUSE button to begin cooking. 7. Serve hot.

Eggs with Beef and Tomato

Prep time: 20 minutes | Cook time: 16 minutes | Serves: 4

Non-stick cooking spray

225g leftover beef, coarsely chopped

2 garlic cloves, pressed

30g kale, torn into pieces and wilted

1 tomato, chopped

4 eggs, beaten

4 tablespoons heavy cream

½ teaspoon turmeric powder

Salt and ground black pepper, to your liking

⅛ teaspoon ground allspice

1. Spritz the inside of four ramekins with a cooking spray. 2. Divide all of the above ingredients among the prepared ramekins. Stir until everything is well combined. 3. Insert the crisper plates in the baskets. Place two ramekins in each basket. 4. Select AIR FRY mode, adjust the cooking temperature to 180°C and set the cooking time to 16 minutes. 5. Press the MATCH COOK button and copy the zone 1 settings to zone 2. 6. Press the START/PAUSE button to begin cooking. You can check the food during cooking. 7. Serve immediately.

Broccoli Fritters

Prep time: 30 minutes | Cook time: 15 minutes | Serves: 6

150g Monterey Jack cheese

1 teaspoon dried dill weed

⅓ teaspoon ground black pepper

3 eggs, whisked

1 teaspoon cayenne pepper

½ teaspoon salt

225g broccoli florets

50g Parmesan cheese

1. Blitz the broccoli florets in a food processor until finely crumbed. 2. Combine the broccoli with the rest of the above ingredients. 3. Roll the mixture into small balls; place the balls in the fridge for approximately half an hour. 4. Insert the crisper plates in the baskets. Divide the croquettes between the baskets in zone 1 and zone 2. 5. Select BAKE mode, adjust the cooking temperature to 170°C and set the cooking time to 15 minutes. 6. Press the MATCH COOK button and copy the zone 1 settings to zone 2. 7. Press the START/PAUSE button to begin cooking. 8. Serve warm.

Cheese Mushroom Balls

Prep time: 30 minutes | Cook time: 25 minutes | Serves: 4

1½ tablespoons olive oil

100g cauliflower florets

3 garlic cloves, peeled and minced

½ yellow onion, finely chopped

1 small-sized red chili pepper, seeded and minced

120ml roasted vegetable stock

200g white mushrooms, finely chopped

Sea salt and ground black pepper, or more to taste

50g Swiss cheese, grated

50g parmesan cheese

1 egg, beaten

1. Blitz the cauliflower florets in your food processor until they're crumbled. 2. Heat the oil in a saucepan over a moderate heat; add the cauliflower, garlic, onions, and chili pepper and cook them until tender. 3. Throw in the mushrooms and fry until they are fragrant and the liquid has almost evaporated. 4. Add the vegetable stock and boil for 18 minutes. 5. Add the salt, black pepper, Swiss cheese, and beaten egg; mix them to combine. 6. Allow the mixture to cool completely. Shape the mixture into balls. Dip the balls in the grated parmesan cheese. 7. Insert the crisper plates in the baskets. Divide the balls between the baskets in zone 1 and zone 2. 8. Select AIR FRY mode, adjust the cooking temperature to 205°C and set the cooking time to 7 minutes. 9. Press the MATCH COOK button and copy the zone 1 settings to zone 2. 10. Press the START/PAUSE button to begin cooking. 11. Serve hot.

Celery & Bacon Croquettes

Prep time: 25 minutes | Cook time: 20 minutes | Serves: 4

2 eggs, lightly beaten

⅓ teaspoon freshly cracked black pepper

100g cheese, grated

½ tablespoon fresh dill, finely chopped

½ tablespoon garlic paste

75 gonion, finely chopped

95g bacon, chopped

2 teaspoons fine sea salt

2 medium-sized celery stalks, trimmed and grated

⅓ teaspoon baking powder

1. Place the celery on a paper towel and squeeze them to remove the excess liquid. 2. Combine the vegetables with the other ingredients in the order listed above. Shape the balls using 1 tablespoon of the vegetable mixture. 3. Gently flatten each ball with your palm or a wide spatula. Spritz the croquettes with cooking oil. 4. Arrange the croquettes into the basket in a single layer. 5. Select BAKE mode, adjust the cooking temperature to 160°C and set the cooking time to 17 minutes. 6. Press the START/PAUSE button to begin cooking. 7. Serve warm with sour cream.

Smoked Tofu Omelet

Prep time: 20 minutes | Cook time: 15 minutes | Serves: 2

2 eggs, beaten

50g cherry tomatoes, chopped

1 pepper, seeded and chopped

⅓ teaspoon freshly ground black pepper

½ purple onion, peeled and sliced

1 teaspoon smoked cayenne pepper

5 medium-sized eggs, well-beaten

90g smoked tofu, crumbled

1 teaspoon seasoned salt

1½ tablespoons fresh chives, chopped

1. Mix up all of the ingredients except the fresh chives in a large bowl. 2. Insert the crisper plate in the basket in zone 1, and transfer the mixture to it. 3. Select AIR FRY mode, adjust the cooking temperature to 160°C and set the cooking time to 15 minutes. 4. Press the START/PAUSE button to begin cooking. 5. Garnish the dish with fresh chopped chives. Enjoy!

Tasty Gruyère Stuffed Mushrooms

Prep time: 20 minutes | Cook time: 15 minutes | Serves: 3

2 garlic cloves, minced

1 teaspoon ground black pepper, or more to taste

½ teaspoon paprika

1 teaspoon dried parsley flakes

1½ tablespoons fresh mint, chopped

1 teaspoon salt, or more to taste

100g Gruyère cheese, shredded

9 large mushrooms, cleaned, stalks removed

1. Mix all of the ingredients except the mushrooms in a mixing bowl to prepare the filling. 2. Stuff the mushrooms with the prepared filling. 3. Insert the crisper plates in the baskets. Divide the stuffed mushrooms between the baskets in zone 1 and zone 2. 4. Select AIR FRY mode, adjust the cooking temperature to 190°C and set the cooking time to 12 minutes. 5. Press the MATCH COOK button and copy the zone 1 settings to zone 2. 6. Press the START/PAUSE button to begin cooking. 7. Taste for doneness and serve at room temperature as an appetizer.

Chicken Sausage Frittata

Prep time: 15 minutes | Cook time: 11 minutes | Serves: 2

1 tablespoon olive oil

2 chicken sausages, sliced

4 eggs

1 garlic clove, minced

½ yellow onion, chopped

Sea salt and ground black pepper, to taste

4 tablespoons Monterey-Jack cheese

1 tablespoon fresh parsley leaves, chopped

1. Transfer the sausages to the basket in zone 1. 2. Select AIR FRY mode, adjust the cooking temperature to 180°C and set the cooking time to 5 minutes. 3. Press the START/PAUSE button to begin cooking. 4. While cooking the sausages, whisk the eggs with garlic and onion in a mixing bowl, and then season them with salt and black pepper. 5. When the cooking time is up, pour the egg mixture over the sausages, top them with cheese, and then resume cooking them for another 6 minutes. 6. Serve immediately with fresh parsley leaves.

Cheese Asparagus Casserole

Prep time: 30 minutes | Cook time: 20 minutes | Serves: 2

65g cauliflower rice

80ml milk

35g cheese, grated

150g white mushrooms, sliced

2 asparagus spears, chopped

1 teaspoon table salt, or to taste

2 well-beaten eggs

⅓ teaspoon smoked cayenne pepper

1 teaspoon ground black pepper, or to taste

⅓ teaspoon dried rosemary, crushed

1. In a mixing dish, thoroughly combine the eggs and milk; stir in ½ of cheese; add the seasonings. 2. Transfer the cauliflower rice to the basket in zone 1, pour ¾ of egg mixture over them and press them gently. 3. Top the cauliflower rice with the mushrooms and chopped asparagus and then pour the remaining egg mixture over the top; make sure to spread it evenly. 4. Top them with the remaining cheese. 5. Select BAKE mode, adjust the cooking temperature to 160°C and set the cooking time to 20 minutes. 6. Press the START/PAUSE button to begin cooking.

Chapter 2 Vegetables and Sides

Chili Cauliflower Florets

Prep time: 5 minutes | Cook time: 15 minutes | Serves: 4

455g cauliflower florets

2 tablespoons sesame oil

2 tablespoons keto hot sauce

3 tablespoons lemon juice

½ teaspoon white pepper

1. Mix sesame oil with lemon juice, hot sauce, and white pepper. 2. Mix cauliflower florets with the lemon juice mixture. 3. Transfer the mixture to the basket. 4. Select ROAST mode, adjust the cooking temperature to 180°C and set the cooking time to 14 minutes. 5. Press the START/PAUSE button to begin cooking. 6. Flip the cauliflower florets halfway through cooking. 7. When the cooking time is up, cook the cauliflower florets at 205°C for 1 minute more. 8. Serve hot.

Cauliflower and Broccoli

Prep time: 5 minutes | Cook time: 15 minutes | Serves: 4

250g broccoli, chopped

250g cauliflower, chopped

100g Jarlsberg cheese, grated

2 tablespoons apple cider vinegar

1 tablespoon avocado oil

1. Mix broccoli with cauliflower, apple cider vinegar, and avocado oil. 2. Transfer the food to the basket in zone 1. 3. Select ROAST mode, adjust the cooking temperature to 180°C and set the cooking time to 15 minutes. 4. Press the START/PAUSE button to begin cooking. 5. Serve warm.

Courgette Noodles

Prep time: 20 minutes | Cook time: 5 minutes | Serves: 4

3 courgettes, trimmed

1 tablespoon coconut oil

25g Parmesan, grated

1. Spiralize the courgettes and mix with coconut oil and Parmesan. 2. Insert the crisper plate in the basket in zone 1, and transfer the mixture to it. 3. Select AIR FRY mode, adjust the cooking temperature to 180°C and set the cooking time to 5 minutes. 4. Press the START/PAUSE button to begin cooking. 5. Carefully mix the cooked noodles.

Coated Jicama Sticks

Prep time: 15 minutes | Cook time: 10 minutes | Serves: 5

375g jicama, peeled, cut into sticks

1 egg, beaten

60g heavy cream

50g coconut shred

1 teaspoon chili powder

Cooking spray

1. Mix egg with heavy cream and chili powder. 2. Dip the jicama sticks in the egg mixture and coat in the coconut shred. 3. Insert the crisper plates in the baskets. Divide the sticks between the baskets in zone 1 and zone 2, and spray them with cooking spray. 4. Select BAKE mode, adjust the cooking temperature to 200°C and set the cooking time to 7 minutes. 5. Press the MATCH COOK button and copy the zone 1 settings to zone 2. 6. Press the START/PAUSE button to begin cooking. 7. When cooked, serve hot.

Spiced Broccoli Steaks

Prep time: 5 minutes | Cook time: 15 minutes | Serves: 4

900g broccoli head

1 tablespoon coconut oil, melted

1 teaspoon garlic powder

½ teaspoon dried oregano

1. Slice the broccoli head into steaks. 2. Rub them with coconut oil, garlic powder, and dried oregano. 3. Insert the crisper plates in the baskets. Divide the broccoli steaks between the baskets in zone 1 and zone 2. 4. Select AIR FRY mode, adjust the cooking temperature to 185°C and set the cooking time to 12 minutes. 5. Press the MATCH COOK button and copy the zone 1 settings to zone 2. 6. Press the START/PAUSE button to begin cooking. 7. Flip the broccoli steaks halfway through the cooking time. 8. Serve hot.

Easy Aubergine Slices

Prep time: 15 minutes | Cook time: 15 minutes | Serves: 2

1 large aubergine, trimmed, peeled

1 teaspoon salt

1 teaspoon minced garlic

Cooking spray

1. Slice the aubergine slices and sprinkle with minced garlic, salt, and cooking spray. 2. Insert the crisper plate in the basket in zone 1, and transfer the egg mixture to it. 3. Select AIR FRY mode, adjust the cooking temperature to 175°C and set the cooking time to 14 minutes. 4. Press the START/PAUSE button to begin cooking. 5. Flip them halfway through the cooking time.

Turmeric Cauliflower Steaks

Prep time: 10 minutes | Cook time: 15 minutes | Serves: 4

675g cauliflower head

1 tablespoon sesame oil

1 teaspoon ground turmeric

1 teaspoon dried dill

1. Cut the cauliflower into the steaks and sprinkle with ground turmeric, dill, and sesame oil. 2. Insert the crisper plates in the baskets. 3. Divide the cauliflower steaks between the baskets in zone 1 and zone 2. 4. Select AIR FRY mode, adjust the cooking temperature to 185°C and set the cooking time to 14 minutes. 5. Press the MATCH COOK button and copy the zone 1 settings to zone 2. 6. Press the START/PAUSE button to begin cooking. 7. Flip the vegetable steaks halfway through cooking. 8. Serve hot.

Garlicky Courgette Slices

Prep time: 10 minutes | Cook time: 6 minutes | Serves: 4

3 large courgettes, sliced

1 tablespoon minced garlic

2 tablespoons sesame oil

1. Mix the sesame oil with minced garlic. 2. Brush the courgette slices with garlic mixture. 3. Insert the crisper plates in the baskets. Divide the courgette slices between the baskets in zone 1 and zone 2. 4. Select AIR FRY mode, adjust the cooking temperature to 205°C and set the cooking time to 6 minutes. 5. Press the MATCH COOK button and copy the zone 1 settings to zone 2. 6. Press the START/PAUSE button to begin cooking. 7. Flip the food halfway through cooking. 8. Serve warm.

Kale in Beef Stock

Prep time: 5 minutes | Cook time: 10 minutes | Serves: 4

90g kale, torn

240ml beef stock

25g almond, chopped

30g mozzarella, shredded

1 teaspoon ghee

1 teaspoon dried oregano

1. Mix up all of the ingredients in a large bowl, and then transfer them to the basket in zone 1. 2. Select ROAST mode, adjust the cooking temperature to 180°C and set the cooking time to 10 minutes. 3. Press the START/PAUSE button to begin cooking. 4. Serve warm.

Trimmed Asparagus

Prep time: 5 minutes | Cook time: 10 minutes | Serves: 4

1 bunch asparagus (approx. 455g), washed and trimmed

⅛ teaspoon dried tarragon, crushed

Salt and pepper

1 to 2 teaspoons extra-light olive oil

1. Spread asparagus spears on cookie sheet or cutting board. 2. Sprinkle the asparagus with tarragon, salt, and pepper. 3. Drizzle with 1 teaspoon of oil and roll the spears or mix by hand. If needed, add up to 1 more teaspoon of oil and mix again until all spears are lightly coated. 4. Insert the crisper plates in the baskets. Divide the food between the baskets in zone 1 and zone 2. 5. Select AIR FRY mode, adjust the cooking temperature to 200°C and set the cooking time to 10 minutes. 6. Press the MATCH COOK button and copy the zone 1 settings to zone 2. 7. Press the START/PAUSE button to begin cooking. 8. Stir the food halfway through cooking. 9. When done, the asparagus spears should be crisp-tender.

Crispy Asparagus Fries

Prep time: 15 minutes | Cook time: 15 minutes | Serves: 4

300g fresh asparagus spears with tough ends trimmed off

2 egg whites

50ml water

80g panko breadcrumbs

25g grated Parmesan cheese, plus 2 tablespoons

¼ teaspoon salt

Oil for misting or cooking spray

1. In a shallow dish, beat egg whites and water until slightly foamy. 2. In another shallow dish, combine panko, Parmesan, and salt. 3. Dip asparagus spears in egg, and then roll in crumbs. Spray them with oil or cooking spray. 4. Insert the crisper plates in the baskets. Divide the asparagus spears between the baskets in zone 1 and zone 2. 5. Select AIR FRY mode, adjust the cooking temperature to 200°C and set the cooking time to 7 minutes. 6. Press the MATCH COOK button and copy the zone 1 settings to zone 2. 7. Press the START/PAUSE button to begin cooking. 8. Serve hot.

Green Beans with Ground Coriander

Prep time: 10 minutes | Cook time: 10 minutes | Serves: 2

300g green beans, roughly chopped

1 tablespoon ground coriander

1 teaspoon salt

1 tablespoon coconut oil, melted

1. Mix green beans with ground coriander, salt, and coconut oil. 2. Divide the green beans between the baskets in zone 1 and zone 2. 3. Select ROAST mode, adjust the cooking temperature to 205°C and set the cooking time to 6 minutes. 4. Press the MATCH COOK button and copy the zone 1 settings to zone 2. 5. Press the START/PAUSE button to begin cooking. 6. Flip the green beans halfway through cooking. 7. Serve and enjoy.

Unseasoned Beetroot

Prep time: 5 minutes | Cook time: 40 minutes | Serves: 4-8

3 large beetroot (about 900g)

1. Cut off leaves, leaving 2.5 cm of stems intact. Do not trim the root tails. 2. Wash beetroot and pat them dry. 3. Insert the crisper plates in the baskets. Divide the beets between the baskets in zone 1 and zone 2. 4. Select AIR FRY mode, adjust the cooking temperature to 200°C and set the cooking time to 40 minutes. 5. Press the MATCH COOK button and copy the zone 1 settings to zone 2. 6. Press the START/PAUSE button to begin cooking. 7. When cooked, cut off the root and stem ends, peel the beets and slice them.

Panko Broccoli Tots

Prep time: 15 minutes | Cook time: 10 minutes | Serves: 4-6

225g broccoli crowns

1 egg, beaten

⅛ teaspoon onion powder

¼ teaspoon salt

⅛ teaspoon pepper

2 tablespoons grated Parmesan cheese

30g panko breadcrumbs

Oil for misting

1. Steam broccoli for 2 minutes. Rinse them in cold water, drain well, and chop finely. 2. In a large bowl, mix broccoli with all other ingredients except the oil. 3. Scoop out small portions of mixture and shape into 24 tots. 4. Insert the crisper plates in the baskets. Divide the tots between the baskets in zone 1 and zone 2. 5. Select AIR FRY mode, adjust the cooking temperature to 200°C and set the cooking time to 10 minutes. 6. Press the MATCH COOK button and copy the zone 1 settings to zone 2. 7. Press the START/PAUSE button to begin cooking. 8. Flip the tots halfway through cooking. 9. Serve hot.

Simple Brussels Sprouts

Prep time: 5 minutes | Cook time: 5 minutes | Serves: 3

1 (250g) package frozen Brussels sprouts, thawed and halved

2 teaspoons olive oil

Salt and pepper

1. Toss the Brussels sprouts and olive oil together. 2. Insert the crisper plates in the baskets. 3. Divide the food between the baskets in zone 1 and zone 2, and season them with salt and pepper. 4. Select AIR FRY mode, adjust the cooking temperature to 180°C and set the cooking time to 5 minutes. 5. Press the MATCH COOK button and copy the zone 1 settings to zone 2. 6. Press the START/PAUSE button to begin cooking. 7. When done, the edges should be lightly browned.

Lemon Pepper-Seasoned Cauliflower

Prep time: 5 minutes | Cook time: 6 minutes | Serves: 4

120ml water

1 (250g) package frozen cauliflower (florets)

1 teaspoon lemon pepper seasoning

1. Pour the water into the basket. 2. Insert the crisper plate in the basket in zone 1, and transfer the cauliflower florets to it, then season them with lemon pepper seasoning. 3. Select AIR FRY mode, adjust the cooking temperature to 200°C and set the cooking time to 5 minutes. 4. Press the START/PAUSE button to begin cooking. 5. Serve hot.

Potato Pot with Sauce

Prep time: 10 minutes | Cook time: 15 minutes | Serves: 4

480g cubed red potatoes (unpeeled, cut into 1 cm cubes)

½ teaspoon garlic powder

Sauce

2 tablespoons milk

1 tablespoon butter

Salt and pepper

1 tablespoon oil

Chopped chives for garnish (optional)

50g sharp Cheddar cheese, grated

1 tablespoon sour cream

1. Place potato cubes in large bowl and sprinkle with garlic, salt, and pepper. Add oil and stir to coat well. 2. Insert the crisper plate in the basket in zone 1, and transfer the potato cubes to it. 3. Select AIR FRY mode, adjust the cooking temperature to 200°C and set the cooking time to 15 minutes. 4. Press the START/PAUSE button to begin cooking. 5. Stir the potato cubes every 5 minutes during cooking. 6. Add the milk and butter to a saucepan, and heat them over medium-low heat; add the cheese and stir until it melts. The melted cheese will remain separated from the milk mixture. 7. When ready to serve, add sour cream to cheese mixture and stir over medium-low heat just until warmed. Place cooked potatoes in serving bowl. Pour sauce over potatoes and stir to combine. 8. Garnish the dish with chives if desired.

Corn Croquettes

Prep time: 10 minutes | Cook time: 15 minutes | Serves: 4

125g leftover mashed potatoes

330g corn kernels (if frozen, thawed, and well drained)

¼ teaspoon onion powder

⅛ teaspoon ground black pepper

¼ teaspoon salt

55g panko breadcrumbs

Oil for misting or cooking spray

1. Place the potatoes and half the corn in food processor and pulse until corn is well chopped. 2. Transfer mixture to large bowl and stir in remaining corn, onion powder, pepper and salt. 3. Shape the mixture into 16 balls. 4. Roll balls in panko crumbs and mist them with oil or cooking spray. 5. Insert the crisper plates in the baskets and line them with parchment paper. Divide the balls between the baskets in zone 1 and zone 2. 6. Select AIR FRY mode, adjust the cooking temperature to 180°C and set the cooking time to 15 minutes. 7. Press the MATCH COOK button and copy the zone 1 settings to zone 2. 8. Press the START/PAUSE button to begin cooking. 9. When done, the balls should be golden brown and crispy.

Fresh Corn on the Cob

Prep time: 5 minutes | Cook time: 15 minutes | Serves: 4

2 large ears fresh corn

Olive oil for misting

Salt (optional)

1. Shuck corn, remove silks, and wash. 2. Cut or break each ear in half crosswise. 3. Spray corn with olive oil. 4. Insert the crisper plate in the basket in zone 1, and transfer the food to it. 5. Select AIR FRY mode, adjust the cooking temperature to 200°C and set the cooking time to 15 minutes. 6. Press the START/PAUSE button to begin cooking. 7. Serve plain or with coarsely ground salt.

Creole Gold Potato Wedges

Prep time: 5 minutes | Cook time: 15 minutes | Serves: 3-4

455g medium Yukon gold potatoes	½ teaspoon salt
½ teaspoon cayenne pepper	½ teaspoon smoked paprika
½ teaspoon thyme	100g dry breadcrumbs
½ teaspoon garlic powder	Oil for misting or cooking spray

1. Wash potatoes, cut them into thick wedges, and drop wedges into a bowl of water to prevent browning. 2. Mix the potato wedges with the cayenne pepper, thyme, garlic powder, salt, paprika, and breadcrumbs and spread on a sheet of wax paper. 3. Remove potatoes from water and, without drying them, roll in the breadcrumb mixture. 4. Insert the crisper plates in the baskets. Divide the potato wedges between the baskets in zone 1 and zone 2. 5. Select AIR FRY mode, adjust the cooking temperature to 200°C and set the cooking time to 15 minutes. 6. Press the MATCH COOK button and copy the zone 1 settings to zone 2. 7. Press the START/PAUSE button to begin cooking. 8. Toss the potato wedges halfway through cooking. You can cook them longer.

Chapter 3 Poultry

Vinegar-Seasoned Chicken Wings

Prep time: 5 minutes | Cook time: 30 minutes | Serves: 4

1 tablespoon olive oil

900g of chicken wings

1 teaspoon ground cinnamon

½ teaspoon apple cider vinegar

1. Sprinkle the chicken wings with ground cinnamon and apple cider vinegar. Coat the chicken wings with olive oil. 2. Insert the crisper plate in the basket in zone 1, and transfer the chicken wings to it. 3. Select AIR FRY mode, adjust the cooking temperature to 190°C and set the cooking time to 30 minutes. 4. Press the START/PAUSE button to begin cooking. 5. Flip the chicken wings halfway through cooking. 6. You can enjoy the dish with salad.

Easy-to-Make Duck Skin

Prep time: 5 minutes | Cook time: 6 minutes | Serves: 6

250g duck skin

1 teaspoon avocado oil

1 teaspoon garlic powder

1. Mix duck skin with avocado oil and garlic powder. 2. Insert the crisper plates in the baskets. 3. Divide the duck skin between the baskets in zone 1 and zone 2. 4. Select AIR FRY mode, adjust the cooking temperature to 205°C and set the cooking time to 6 minutes. 5. Press the MATCH COOK button and copy the zone 1 settings to zone 2. 6. Press the START/PAUSE button to begin cooking. 7. Flip the duck skin halfway through cooking.

Coconut Chicken Breast

Prep time: 5 minutes | Cook time: 20 minutes | Serves: 4

900g chicken breast, skinless, boneless

50g coconut shred

2 eggs, beaten

1 teaspoon Italian seasonings

1. Cut the chicken breast into tenders and sprinkle with Italian seasonings. 2. Dip the chicken tenders in the eggs and coat in the coconut shred. 3. Insert the crisper plate in the basket in zone 1, and transfer the chicken tenders to it. 4. Select AIR FRY mode, adjust the cooking temperature to 190°C and set the cooking time to 20 minutes. 5. Press the START/PAUSE button to begin cooking. 6. Flip the chicken tenders halfway through cooking.

Mustard Marinated Chicken

Prep time: 30 minutes | Cook time: 26 minutes | Serves: 4

½ teaspoon stone-ground mustard

½ teaspoon minced fresh oregano

80ml freshly squeezed lime juice

2 small-sized chicken breasts, skin-on

1 teaspoon salt

1 teaspoon freshly cracked mixed peppercorns

1. Toss all of the above ingredients in a medium-sized mixing dish; marinate the chicken breasts overnight. 2. Insert the crisper plate in the basket in zone 1, and transfer the chicken breasts to it. 3. Select AIR FRY mode, adjust the cooking temperature to 175°C and set the cooking time to 26 minutes. 4. Press the START/PAUSE button to begin cooking. 5. Serve warm.

Sweet-Sour Chicken Drumsticks

Prep time: 10 minutes | Cook time: 30 minutes | Serves: 4

1 tablespoon keto tomato paste

2 tablespoons avocado oil

2 tablespoons coconut aminos

1 teaspoon garlic powder

1 teaspoon chili flakes

900g chicken drumsticks

1 teaspoon Erythritol

1. Coat the chicken drumsticks with tomato paste, avocado oil, coconut aminos, garlic powder, chili flakes, and Erythritol. 2. Insert the crisper plate in the basket in zone 1, and transfer the chicken drumsticks to it. 3. Select AIR FRY mode, adjust the cooking temperature to 180°C and set the cooking time to 30 minutes. 4. Press the START/PAUSE button to begin cooking. 5. Flip the chicken drumsticks halfway through cooking.

Skinless Chicken Thighs

Prep time: 10 minutes | Cook time: 15 minutes | Serves: 4

400g chicken thighs, skinless

1 teaspoon chili powder

80ml apple cider vinegar

1 tablespoon avocado oil

1. Coat the chicken thighs with chili powder, apple cider vinegar, and avocado oil. 2. Insert the crisper plates in the baskets. 3. Divide the chicken thighs between the baskets in zone 1 and zone 2. 4. Select AIR FRY mode, adjust the cooking temperature to 190°C and set the cooking time to 15 minutes. 5. Press the MATCH COOK button and copy the zone 1 settings to zone 2. 6. Press the START/PAUSE button to begin cooking. 7. Serve hot.

Tarragon-Seasoned Chicken Thighs

Prep time: 5 minutes | Cook time: 30 minutes | Serves: 4

900g chicken thighs

1 tablespoon dried tarragon

1 tablespoon avocado oil

½ teaspoon salt

1. Mix chicken thighs with dried tarragon, avocado oil, and salt. 2. Insert the crisper plate in the basket in zone 1, and transfer the chicken thighs to it. 3. Select AIR FRY mode, adjust the cooking temperature to 180°C and set the cooking time to 30 minutes. 4. Press the START/PAUSE button to begin cooking. 5. Flip the chicken thighs halfway through cooking.

Nutty Turkey Breast

Prep time: 30 minutes | Cook time: 28 minutes | Serves: 2

1½ tablespoons coconut aminos

½ tablespoon xanthan gum

2 bay leaves

80ml dry sherry

1½ tablespoons chopped walnuts

1 teaspoon shallot powder

455g turkey breasts, sliced

1 teaspoon garlic powder

2 teaspoons olive oil

½ teaspoon onion salt

½ teaspoon red pepper flakes, crushed

1 teaspoon ground black pepper

1. Mix all of the ingredients, minus chopped walnuts, in a mixing bowl and let them marinate for at least 1 hour. 2. Insert the crisper plate in the basket in zone 1, and transfer the turkey slices to it. 3. Select AIR FRY mode, adjust the cooking temperature to 200°C and set the cooking time to 28 minutes. 4. Press the START/PAUSE button to begin cooking. 5. Top the food with chopped walnuts after 23 minutes of cooking time. 6. When cooked, serve hot.

Eggs & Sausage Keto Rolls

Prep time: 40 minutes | Cook time: 26 minutes | Serves: 6

1 teaspoon dried dill weed

1 teaspoon mustard seeds

6 turkey sausages

3 peppers, seeded and thinly sliced

6 medium-sized eggs

½ teaspoon fennel seeds

1 teaspoon sea salt

⅓ teaspoon freshly cracked pink peppercorns

For Keto Rolls

120g ricotta cheese, crumbled

120g part-skim mozzarella cheese, shredded

1 egg

60g coconut flour

50g almond flour

1 teaspoon baking soda

2 tablespoons plain whey protein isolate

1. Crack the eggs into the ramekins, and sprinkle them with salt, dill weed, mustard seeds, fennel seeds, and cracked peppercorns. 2. Insert the crisper plates in the baskets. 3 Place the sausages and peppers in zone 1, and add the egg ramekins to zone 2. 4. Select AIR FRY mode, adjust the cooking temperature to 160°C and set the cooking time to 8 minutes. 5. Select zone 2, set the BAKE mode, and adjust the cooking temperature to 200°C and cooking time to 12 minutes. 6. Press the SMART FINISH button, and then press the START/PAUSE button to begin cooking. 7. To make the keto rolls, microwave the cheese for 1 minute 30 seconds, stirring twice. Add the cheese to the bowl of a food processor and blend well. Fold in the egg and mix again. 8. Add in the flour, baking soda, and plain when protein isolates; blend again. Scrape the batter onto the centre of a lightly greased cling film. 9. Form the dough into a disk and transfer to your freezer to cool, and then cut the dough into 6 pieces. 10. Insert the crisper plate in the basket in zone 1, line it with parchment paper and transfer the pieces to it. 11. Select BAKE mode, adjust the cooking temperature to 205°C and set the cooking time to 14 minutes. 12. Press the START/PAUSE button to begin cooking. 13. Serve eggs and sausages on keto rolls and enjoy!

Bacon-Wrapped Turkey

Prep time: 20 minutes | Cook time: 15 minutes | Serves: 12

1½ small-sized turkey breasts, chop into 12 pieces

12 thin slices Asiago cheese

Paprika, to taste

Fine sea salt and ground black pepper, to savor

12 rashers bacon

1. Lay out the bacon rashers; place 1 slice of Asiago cheese on each bacon piece. 2. Top them with turkey, season with paprika, salt, and pepper, and roll them up; secure with a cocktail stick. 3. Insert the crisper plates in the baskets, and transfer the food to it. 4. Select AIR FRY mode, adjust the cooking temperature to 185°C and set the cooking time to 13 minutes. 5. Press the MATCH COOK button and copy the zone 1 settings to zone 2. 6. Press the START/PAUSE button to begin cooking. 7. Serve hot.

Typical Chicken Nuggets

Prep time: 20 minutes | Cook time: 10 minutes | Serves: 4

675g chicken tenderloins, cut into small pieces

½ teaspoon garlic salt

½ teaspoon cayenne pepper

¼ teaspoon black pepper, freshly cracked

4 tablespoons olive oil

2 scoops low-carb unflavoured protein powder

4 tablespoons Parmesan cheese, freshly grated

1. Season each piece of the chicken with garlic salt, cayenne pepper, and black pepper. 2. In a mixing bowl, thoroughly combine the olive oil with protein powder and parmesan cheese. 3. Dip each piece of chicken in the parmesan mixture. 4. Insert the crisper plates in the baskets. Divide the batter between the baskets in zone 1 and zone 2. 5. Select AIR FRY mode, adjust the cooking temperature to 200°C and set the cooking time to 8 minutes. 6. Press the MATCH COOK button and copy the zone 1 settings to zone 2. 7. Press the START/PAUSE button to begin cooking. 8. Serve hot.

Aromatic Turkey Breast

Prep time: 60 minutes | Cook time: 55 minutes | Serves: 4

½ teaspoon dried thyme

675g turkey breasts

½ teaspoon dried sage

3 whole star anise

1½ tablespoons olive oil

1½ tablespoons hot mustard

1 teaspoon smoked cayenne pepper

1 teaspoon fine sea salt

1. Brush the turkey breast with olive oil and sprinkle with seasonings. 2. Insert the crisper plate in the basket in zone 1, and transfer the turkey breast to it. 3. Select AIR FRY mode, adjust the cooking temperature to 185°C and set the cooking time to 53 minutes. 4. Press the START/PAUSE button to begin cooking. 5. Spread the cooked breast with the hot mustard after 45 minutes of cooking time. 6. Let the dish rest before slicing and serving.

Pepper Chicken Cutlets

Prep time: 10 minutes | Cook time: 16 minutes | Serves: 4

900g chicken fillet

1 teaspoon ground black pepper

1 teaspoon coconut oil, melted

1 teaspoon chili powder

1. Sprinkle the chicken fillets with ground black pepper and chili powder. 2. Insert the crisper plate in the basket in zone 1, and transfer the chicken fillet to it. 3. Spray the chicken fillet with coconut oil. 4. Select AIR FRY mode, adjust the cooking temperature to 190°C and set the cooking time to 16 minutes. 5. Press the START/PAUSE button to begin cooking. 6. Flip the chicken fillet halfway through cooking.

Thanksgiving Turkey

Prep time: 50 minutes | Cook time: 50 minutes | Serves: 6

2 teaspoons butter, softened

1 teaspoon dried sage

2 sprigs rosemary, chopped

1 teaspoon salt

¼ teaspoon freshly ground black pepper, or more to taste

1 whole turkey breast

2 tablespoons turkey stock

2 tablespoons whole-grain mustard

1 tablespoon butter

1. Combine 2 tablespoons of butter, sage, rosemary, salt, and pepper; spread the mixture evenly over the surface of the turkey breast. 2. Insert the crisper plates in the baskets. 3. Divide the meat between the baskets in zone 1 and zone 2. 4. Select ROAST mode, adjust the cooking temperature to 180°C and set the cooking time to 48 minutes. 5. Press the MATCH COOK button and copy the zone 1 settings to zone 2. 6. Press the START/PAUSE button to begin cooking. 7. Flip the chicken breast halfway through cooking. 8. Flip the turkey breast after 20 minutes of cooking time and after 36 minutes of cooking time respectively. 9. While the turkey is roasting, whisk the other ingredients in a saucepan. After that, spread the gravy all over the turkey breast. 10. Let the turkey rest for a few minutes before carving.

Loaded Turkey Meatloaf

Prep time: 50 minutes | Cook time: 50 minutes | Serves: 6

900g turkey mince

80g spring onions, finely chopped

2 garlic cloves, finely minced

1 teaspoon dried thyme

½ teaspoon dried basil

75g cheese, shredded

1 tablespoon tamari sauce

Salt and black pepper, to your liking

60g roasted red pepper tomato sauce

¾ tablespoons olive oil

1 medium-sized egg, well beaten

1. Sauté the turkey mince, spring onions, garlic, thyme, and basil in a frying pan over medium heat until just tender and fragrant. 2. Combine sautéed mixture with the cheese and tamari sauce; then form the mixture into a loaf shape. 3. Mix the remaining items and pour them over the meatloaf. 4. Insert the crisper plate in the basket in zone 1, and transfer the loaf to it. 5. Select AIR FRY mode, adjust the cooking temperature to 180°C and set the cooking time to 47 minutes. 6. Press the START/PAUSE button to begin cooking. 7. Serve warm.

Tangy Chicken with Parsley

Prep time: 30 minutes | Cook time: 26 minutes | Serves: 2

1½ handful fresh parsley, roughly chopped

Fresh juice of ½ lime

1 teaspoon ground black pepper

1½ large-sized chicken breasts, cut into halves

1 teaspoon salt

Zest of ½ lime

1. Toss the chicken breasts with the other ingredients and let it marinate a couple of hours. 2. Insert the crisper plate in the basket in zone 1, and transfer the chicken breasts to it. 3. Select ROAST mode, adjust the cooking temperature to 170°C and set the cooking time to 26 minutes. 4. Press the START/PAUSE button to begin cooking. 5. Serve warm.

Chicken with Smoked Bacon

Prep time: 50 minutes | Cook time: 20 minutes | Serves: 2

4 rashers smoked bacon

2 chicken filets

½ teaspoon coarse sea salt

¼ teaspoon black pepper, preferably freshly ground

1 teaspoon garlic, minced

1 (5cm) piece ginger, peeled and minced

1 teaspoon black mustard seeds

1 teaspoon mild curry powder

120ml coconut milk

50g Parmesan cheese, grated

1. In a mixing bowl, place the chicken fillets, salt, black pepper, garlic, ginger, mustard seeds, curry powder, and milk. Let it marinate in your refrigerator about 30 minutes. 2. In another bowl, place the grated parmesan cheese. 3. Dredge the chicken fillets through the parmesan mixture. 4. Insert the crisper plates in the baskets. 5. Place the smoked bacon in zone 1 and add the chicken fillets to zone 2. 6. Select AIR FRY mode, adjust the cooking temperature to 205°C and set the cooking time to 7 minutes. 7. Select zone 2, set the AIR FRY mode, and adjust the cooking temperature to 190°C and cooking time to 12 minutes. 8. Press the SMART FINISH button, and then press the START/PAUSE button to begin cooking. 9. Flip the chicken fillets halfway through cooking. 10. Serve and enjoy!

Turkey Thighs with Vegetables

Prep time: 1 hour 15 minutes | Cook time: 45 minutes | Serves: 4

- 1 red onion, cut into wedges
- 1 carrot, trimmed and sliced
- 1 celery stalk, trimmed and sliced
- 90g Brussels sprouts, trimmed and halved
- 240ml roasted vegetable stock
- 1 tablespoon apple cider vinegar
- 4 turkey thighs
- ½ teaspoon mixed peppercorns, freshly cracked
- 1 teaspoon fine sea salt
- 1 teaspoon cayenne pepper
- 1 teaspoon onion powder
- ½ teaspoon garlic powder
- ⅓ teaspoon mustard seeds

1. Place the vegetables on the bottom of a suitable baking dish and pour in roasted vegetable stock. 2. Mix all of the remaining ingredients in a large bowl and marinate the turkey thighs for 30 minutes, and then lay them on the top of the vegetables. 3. Transfer the baking dish to the basket in zone 1. 4. Select ROAST mode, adjust the cooking temperature to 165°C and set the cooking time to 45 minutes. 5. Press the START/PAUSE button to begin cooking. 6. Serve warm.

Chicken with Leeks

Prep time: 20 minutes | Cook time: 20 minutes | Serves: 6

2 leeks, sliced

2 large-sized tomatoes, chopped

3 cloves garlic, minced

½ teaspoon dried oregano

6 chicken legs, boneless and skinless

½ teaspoon smoked cayenne pepper

2 tablespoons olive oil

A freshly ground nutmeg

1. In a mixing dish, thoroughly combine all ingredients, minus the leeks. Place the mixture in the refrigerator and let it marinate overnight. 2. Transfer the mixture to the basket in zone 1. 3. Select ROAST mode, adjust the cooking temperature to 190°C and set the cooking time to 18 minutes. 4. Press the START/PAUSE button to begin cooking. 5. Turn the food halfway through cooking. 6. Serve the dish with hoisin sauce.

Chicken Sliders in Chili Sauce

Prep time: 20 minutes | Cook time: 20 minutes | Serves: 4

⅓ teaspoon paprika

60g spring onions, peeled and chopped

3 cloves garlic, peeled and minced

1 teaspoon ground black pepper, or to taste

½ teaspoon fresh basil, minced

210g chicken, minced

1½ tablespoons coconut aminos

½ teaspoon grated fresh ginger

½ tablespoon chili sauce

1 teaspoon salt

1. Thoroughly combine all ingredients in a mixing dish. 2. Form the mixture into 4 patties. 3. Insert the crisper plate in the basket in zone 1, and transfer the patties to it. 4. Select AIR FRY mode, adjust the cooking temperature to 180°C and set the cooking time to 18 minutes. 5. Press the START/PAUSE button to begin cooking. 6. Garnish the dish with toppings of choice.

Italian-Style Chicken Breasts

Prep time: 20 minutes | Cook time: 11 minutes | Serves: 4

50g Asiago cheese, cut into sticks

80g tomato paste

½ teaspoon garlic paste

2 chicken breasts cut in half lengthwise

60g springonions, chopped

1 tablespoon chili sauce

120ml roasted vegetable stock

1 tablespoon sesame oil

1 teaspoon salt

2 teaspoons unsweetened cocoa

½ teaspoon sweet paprika, or more to taste

1. Sprinkle chicken breasts with the salt and sweet paprika, drizzle them with chili sauce and then place a stick of Asiago cheese in the middle of each chicken breast. 2. Tie the whole thing using a kitchen string; give a drizzle of sesame oil. 3. Insert the crisper plate in the basket in zone 1, and transfer the chicken breasts to it, and place in the remaining ingredients. 4. Select AIR FRY mode, adjust the cooking temperature to 200°C and set the cooking time to 11 minutes. 5. Press the START/PAUSE button to begin cooking. 6. Garnish the dish with fresh or pickled salad, and enjoy.

Rustic Turkey Breasts

Prep time: 50 minutes | Cook time: 50 minutes | Serves: 4

675g turkey breasts, boneless and skinless

½ palmful chopped fresh sage leaves

1½ tablespoons freshly squeezed lemon juice

⅓ teaspoon dry mustard

80ml dry white wine

3 cloves garlic, minced

2 leeks cut into thick slices

½ teaspoon smoked paprika

2 tablespoons olive oil

1. Combine sage leaves, lemon juice, mustard, garlic, and paprika in a small-sized mixing bowl; mix thoroughly until everything is well combined. 2. Smear this mixture on the turkey breast. Add white wine and let it marinate for about 2 hours. 3. Insert the crisper plate in the basket in zone 1, and transfer the turkey breasts to it along with the leeks. 4. Drizzle the food in the basket with olive oil. 5. Select BAKE mode, adjust the cooking temperature to 190°C and set the cooking time to 48 minutes. 6. Press the START/PAUSE button to begin cooking. 7. Flip the turkey breasts once or twice during cooking. 8. Serve hot.

Chapter 4 Beef, Pork, and Lamb

T-Bone Steak with Aromatics

Prep time: 20 minutes | Cook time: 15 minutes | Serves: 3

455g T-bone steak

4 garlic cloves, halved

2 tablespoons olive oil

60ml tamari sauce

4 tablespoons tomato paste

1 teaspoon Sriracha sauce

2 tablespoons white vinegar

1 teaspoon dried rosemary

½ teaspoon dried basil

2 heaping tablespoons coriander, chopped

1. Rub the garlic halves all over the T-bone steak. 2. Drizzle the oil all over the steak and transfer it to the grill pan. 3. Insert the crisper plate in the basket in zone 1, and transfer the steak to it. 4. Select ROAST mode, adjust the cooking temperature to 205°C and set the cooking time to 15 minutes. 5. Press the START/PAUSE button to begin cooking. 6. Whisk the tamari sauce, tomato paste, Sriracha, vinegar, rosemary, and basil, and pour the mixture over the steak after 10 minutes of cooking time. 7. Serve garnished with fresh coriander.

Tangy Beef Strips

Prep time: 20 minutes | Cook time: 15 minutes | Serves: 4

675g sirloin steak

60ml red wine

60ml fresh lime juice

1 teaspoon garlic powder

1 teaspoon shallot powder

1 teaspoon celery seeds

1 teaspoon mustard seeds

Coarse sea salt and ground black pepper, to taste

1 teaspoon red pepper flakes

2 eggs, lightly whisked

100g parmesan cheese

1 teaspoon paprika

1. Place the steak, red wine, lime juice, garlic powder, shallot powder, celery seeds, mustard seeds, salt, black pepper, and red pepper in a large ceramic bowl; let it marinate for 3 hours. 2. Tenderize the cube steak by pounding with a mallet; cut into 2.5 cm strips. 3. In a shallow bowl, whisk the eggs. In another bowl, mix the parmesan cheese and paprika. 4. Dip the beef pieces into the whisked eggs and coat on all sides. Dredge the beef pieces in the parmesan mixture. 5. Insert the crisper plate in the basket in zone 1, and transfer the beef pieces to it. 6. Select AIR FRY mode, adjust the cooking temperature to 205°C and set the cooking time to 14 minutes. 7. Press the START/PAUSE button to begin cooking. 8. Flip the beef pieces halfway through cooking. 9. Make the sauce by heating the reserved marinade in a saucepan over medium heat; let it simmer until thoroughly warmed. Serve the steak fingers with the sauce on the side. Enjoy!

Lemony Beef Steaks

Prep time: 25 minutes | Cook time: 20 minutes | Serves: 2

455g beef steaks

4 tablespoons white wine

2 teaspoons crushed coriander seeds

½ teaspoon fennel seeds

80ml beef stock

2 tablespoons lemon zest, grated

2 tablespoons rapeseed oil

½ lemon, cut into wedges

Salt flakes and freshly ground black pepper, to taste

1. Heat the oil in a saucepan over a moderate flame; cook the garlic for 1 minute or until just fragrant. 2. Remove the pan from the heat; add the beef stock, wine, lemon zest, coriander seeds, fennel, salt flakes, and freshly ground black. Pour the mixture into a baking dish. 3. Add beef steaks to the baking dish; toss to coat well. 4. Tuck the lemon wedges among the beef steaks. 5. Insert the crisper plate in the basket in zone 1, and transfer the steaks to it. 6. Select AIR FRY mode, adjust the cooking temperature to 180°C and set the cooking time to 18 minutes. 7. Press the START/PAUSE button to begin cooking. 8. Serve warm.

Beef Chops with Coriander

Prep time: 35 minutes | Cook time: 30 minutes | Serves: 3

- 1½ teaspoons English mustard
- 3 boneless beef chops
- ⅓ teaspoon garlic pepper
- 2 teaspoons oregano, dried
- 2 tablespoons vegetable oil
- 1½ tablespoons fresh coriander, chopped
- ½ teaspoon onion powder
- ½ teaspoon basil, dried
- Grated rind of ½ small-sized lime
- ½ teaspoon fine sea salt

1. Mix all of the ingredients except the chops and the new potatoes. 2. Evenly spread the beef chops with the English mustard rub. 3. Insert the crisper plate in the basket in zone 1. 4. Place the new potatoes on the crisper plate, and top them with the beef chops. 5. Select AIR FRY mode, adjust the cooking temperature to 185°C and set the cooking time to 27 minutes. 6. Press the START/PAUSE button to begin cooking. 7. Flip the beef chops halfway through cooking. 8. Serve on individual plates with a keto salad on the side, if desired.

Beef Chops with Salad

Prep time: 15 minutes | Cook time: 15 minutes | Serves: 2

120ml vegetable stock

65g spring onions, chopped

1 cloves garlic, minced

For the Salad

1½ tablespoons freshly grated Parmesan

1 tablespoon apple cider vinegar

2 tablespoons extra-virgin olive oil

2 beef chops

½ tablespoon melted butter

Table salt and ground black pepper, to savor

60g very finely chopped or slivered curly kale

⅓ teaspoon ground black pepper, or more to taste

1 teaspoon table salt

1. Toss beef chops with salt, pepper, butter, spring onions, and garlic in the basket; pour in the stock; gently stir to coat. 2. Select ROAST mode, adjust the cooking temperature to 200°C and set the cooking time to 14 minutes. 3. Press the START/PAUSE button to begin cooking. 4. Make the parmesan-kale salad by mixing all salad components. 5. Serve beef chops with the prepared kale salad.

Beef with Pearl Onions and Cauliflower

Prep time: 20 minutes | Cook time: 12 minutes | Serves: 4

675g New York strip, cut into strips

1 (455g) head cauliflower, broken into florets

Marinade:

1 tablespoon olive oil

2 cloves garlic, minced

1 teaspoon of ground ginger

120g pearl onion, sliced

60g tomato paste

120ml red wine

1. Mix all ingredients for the marinade. Add the beef to the marinade and let it sit in the refrigerator for 1 hour. 2. Insert the crisper plate in the basket in zone 1; transfer the meat, cauliflower and onions to it, and drizzle a few tablespoons of marinade over the food. 3. Select AIR FRY mode, adjust the cooking temperature to 205°C and set the cooking time to 12 minutes. 4. Press the START/PAUSE button to begin cooking. 5. Toss the food halfway through cooking. 6. Serve warm.

Teriyaki Steak

Prep time: 40 minutes | Cook time: 40 minutes | Serves: 4

2 heaping tablespoons fresh parsley, roughly chopped

455g beef rump steaks

2 heaping tablespoons fresh chives, roughly chopped

Salt and black pepper (or mixed peppercorns), to savor

For the Sauce

60ml rice vinegar

1 tablespoon fresh ginger, grated

1½ tablespoons mirin

3 garlic cloves, minced

2 tablespoon rice bran oil

80ml soy sauce

A few drops of liquid Stevia

1. Steam the beef rump steaks for 8 minutes in a deep frying pan . 2. Season the beef rump steaks with salt and black pepper; scatter the chopped parsley and chives over the top. 3. Insert the crisper plate in the basket in zone 1, and transfer the beef rump steaks to it. 4. Select ROAST mode, adjust the cooking temperature to 175°C and set the cooking time to 28 minutes. 5. Press the START/PAUSE button to begin cooking. 6. Flip the beef rump steaks halfway through cooking. 7. Simmer the ingredients for the teriyaki sauce in a sauté pan until the sauce has thickened. 8. Toss the beef with the teriyaki sauce until it is well covered and serve. Enjoy!

Beef Bulgogi Burgers

Prep time: 20 minutes | Cook time: 18 minutes | Serves: 4

675g beef mince

1 teaspoon garlic, minced

2 tablespoons spring onions, chopped

Sea salt and cracked black pepper, to taste

1 teaspoon Gochugaru (Korean chili powder)

½ teaspoon dried marjoram

1 teaspoon dried thyme

1 teaspoon mustard seeds

½ teaspoon shallot powder

½ teaspoon cumin powder

½ teaspoon paprika

1 tablespoon liquid smoke flavouring

1. In a mixing bowl, thoroughly combine all ingredients until well combined. 2. Shape into four patties and spritz them with cooking oil on both sides. 3. Transfer the food to the basket in zone 1. 4. Select BAKE mode, adjust the cooking temperature to 180°C and set the cooking time to 18 minutes. 5. Press the START/PAUSE button to begin cooking. 6. Toss the food halfway through cooking. 7. Serve warm.

Beer-Braised Beef

Prep time: 20 minutes | Cook time: 15 minutes | Serves: 4

675g short loin

2 tablespoons olive oil

2-3 cloves garlic, finely minced

180g leeks, sliced

1 bottle beer

1 rosemary sprig

2 thyme sprigs

1 teaspoon mustard seeds

1 bay leaf

1. Pat the beef dry; then, tenderize the beef with a meat mallet to soften the fibres. Place it in a large-sized mixing dish. 2. Add the remaining ingredients; toss to coat well and let it marinate for at least 1 hour. 3. Transfer the mixture to the basket in zone 1. 4. Select AIR FRY mode, adjust the cooking temperature to 200°C and set the cooking time to 15 minutes. 5. Press the START/PAUSE button to begin cooking. 6. Flip the meat halfway through cooking. 7. Serve warm.

Asian Steak Strips

Prep time: 40 minutes | Cook time: 30 minutes | Serves: 4

900g top round steak, cut into bite-sized strips

2 garlic cloves, sliced

1 teaspoon dried marjoram

60ml red wine

1 tablespoon tamari sauce

Salt and black pepper, to taste

1 tablespoon olive oil

1 red onion, sliced

2 peppers, sliced

1 celery stalk, sliced

1. Place the top round, garlic, marjoram, red wine, tamari sauce, salt and pepper in a bowl, cover the bowl and let the food marinate for 1 hour. 2. Insert the crisper plate in the basket in zone 1, and transfer the beef strips without the marinade to it. 3. Select AIR FRY mode, adjust the cooking temperature to 180°C and set the cooking time to 30 minutes. 4. Press the START/PAUSE button to begin cooking. 5. Add the onion, peppers, carrot, and garlic halfway through cooking. Baste the meat with the marinade every 5 minutes. 6. Serve warm.

Spicy Steak Pieces

Prep time: 25 minutes | Cook time: 20 minutes | Serves: 4

455g flank steak, cut into small pieces

1 teaspoon fresh sage leaves, minced

80ml olive oil

3 teaspoons sesame oil

3 tablespoons Shaoxing wine

2 tablespoons tamari

1 teaspoon hot sauce

⅛ teaspoon xanthum gum

1 teaspoon seasoned salt

3 cloves garlic, minced

1 teaspoon fresh rosemary leaves, finely minced

½ teaspoon freshly cracked black pepper

1. Heat the oil in a sauté pan over a moderate heat; sauté the garlic until just tender and fragrant. 2. Toss in the remaining ingredients. 3. Transfer the mixture to the basket in zone 1. 4. Select ROAST mode, adjust the cooking temperature to 175°C and set the cooking time to 18 minutes. 5. Press the START/PAUSE button to begin cooking. 6. Serve warm.

Filet Mignon with Peanut Sauce

Prep time: 25 minutes | Cook time: 20 minutes | Serves: 4

900g filet mignon, sliced into bite-sized strips

1 tablespoon oyster sauce

2 tablespoons sesame oil

2 tablespoons tamari sauce

1 tablespoon ginger-garlic paste

1 tablespoon mustard

1 teaspoon chili powder

65g peanut butter

2 tablespoons lime juice

1 teaspoon red pepper flakes

2 tablespoons water

1. Place the beef strips, oyster sauce, sesame oil, tamari sauce, ginger-garlic paste, mustard, and chili powder in a large ceramic dish. 2. Cover the dish and allow it to marinate for 2 hours in the refrigerator. 3. Transfer the egg mixture to the basket in zone 1. 4. Select AIR FRY mode, adjust the cooking temperature to 205°C and set the cooking time to 18 minutes. 5. Press the START/PAUSE button to begin cooking. 6. Toss the food occasionally. 7. Mix the peanut butter with lime juice, red pepper flakes, and water. Spoon the sauce onto the cooked beef strips and serve warm.

Rich Meatloaf

Prep time: 35 minutes | Cook time: 15 minutes | Serves: 5

- 455g beef, minced
- 225g veal, minced
- 1 egg
- 4 tablespoons vegetable juice
- 50g parmesan, grated
- 2 peppers, chopped
- 1 onion, chopped
- 2 garlic cloves, minced
- 2 tablespoons tomato paste
- 2 tablespoons soy sauce
- 1 (25g) package ranch dressing mix
- Sea salt, to taste
- ½ teaspoon ground black pepper, to taste
- 175g tomato puree
- 1 tablespoon Dijon mustard

1. In a mixing bowl, thoroughly combine the beef mince, veal, egg, vegetable juice, parmesan, peppers, onion, garlic, tomato paste, soy sauce, ranch dressing mix, salt, and ground black pepper. 2. Mix until everything is well incorporated and press into a lightly greased meatloaf pan. 3. Transfer the pan to the basket in zone 1. 4. Select BAKE mode, adjust the cooking temperature to 165°C and set the cooking time to 27 minutes. 5. Press the START/PAUSE button to begin cooking. 6. Whisk the tomato puree with the mustard and spread them over the meatloaf after 25 minutes of cooking time. 7. Let the dish stand on a cooling rack for 6 minutes before slicing and serving.

Spicy Steak

Prep time: 20 minutes | Cook time: 15 minutes | Serves: 2

½ Ancho chili pepper, soaked in hot water before using

1 tablespoon brandy

2 teaspoons smoked paprika

1½ tablespoons olive oil

2 beef steaks

Salt, to taste

1 teaspoon ground allspice

3 cloves garlic, sliced

1. Sprinkle the beef steaks with salt, paprika, and allspice. Scatter the sliced garlic over the top. 2. Drizzle the steak with brandy and olive oil; spread minced Ancho chili pepper over the top. 3. Insert the crisper plate in the basket in zone 1, and transfer the food to it. 4. Select BAKE mode, adjust the cooking temperature to 195°C and set the cooking time to 14 minutes. 5. Press the START/PAUSE button to begin cooking. 6. Flip the steaks halfway through cooking. 7. Serve warm.

Beef Tenderloins in Beef Stock

Prep time: 1 hour 5 minutes | Cook time: 25 minutes | Serves: 2

80ml beef stock

2 tablespoons Cajun seasoning, crushed

½ teaspoon garlic powder

340g beef tenderloins

½ tablespoon pear cider vinegar

⅓ teaspoon cayenne pepper

1½ tablespoon olive oil

½ teaspoon freshly ground black pepper

1 teaspoon salt

1. Coat the beef tenderloins with salt, cayenne pepper, and black pepper. 2. Mix the remaining items in a medium-sized bowl; let the meat marinate for 40 minutes in this mixture. 3. Transfer the food to the basket in zone 1. 4. Select ROAST mode, adjust the cooking temperature to 195°C and set the cooking time to 22 minutes. 5. Press the START/PAUSE button to begin cooking. 6. Flip the food halfway through cooking. 7. Serve warm.

Meatballs with Spicy Sauce

Prep time: 20 minutes | Cook time: 15 minutes | Serves: 4

4 tablespoons parmesan, grated

60g green onion

455g beef sausage meat

For the Sauce

2 tablespoons Worcestershire sauce

⅓ yellow onion, minced

Dash of Tabasco sauce

3 garlic cloves, minced

⅓ teaspoon ground black pepper

Sea salt, to taste

60g tomato paste

1 teaspoon cumin powder

½ tablespoon balsamic vinegar

1. Knead all of the above ingredients until everything is well incorporated. 2. Roll the mixture into balls. 3. Insert the crisper plate in the basket in zone 1, and transfer the meatballs to it. 4. Select AIR FRY mode, adjust the cooking temperature to 185°C and set the cooking time to 13 minutes. 5. Press the START/PAUSE button to begin cooking. 6. In a saucepan, cook the ingredients for the sauce until thoroughly warmed. 7. Serve the meatballs with the tomato sauce.

Filet Mignon Steaks

Prep time: 25 minutes | Cook time: 25 minutes | Serves: 6

40g butter, at room temperature

120g heavy cream

½ medium-sized garlic bulb, peeled and pressed

6 filet mignon steaks

2 teaspoons mixed peppercorns, freshly cracked

1½ tablespoons apple cider

A dash of hot sauce

1½ teaspoons sea salt flakes

1. Season the mignon steaks with the cracked peppercorns and salt flakes. 2. Insert the crisper plates in the baskets. 3. Divide the mignon steaks between the baskets in zone 1 and zone 2. 4. Select ROAST mode, adjust the cooking temperature to 195°C and set the cooking time to 24 minutes. 5. Press the MATCH COOK button and copy the zone 1 settings to zone 2. 6. Press the START/PAUSE button to begin cooking. 7. Flip the steaks halfway through cooking. 8. In a small nonstick saucepan that is placed over a moderate flame, mash the garlic to a smooth paste. Whisk in the rest of the above ingredients. Whisk constantly until it has a uniform consistency. 9. Lay the filet mignon steaks on serving plates; spoon a little sauce onto each filet mignon. Enjoy.

Whisky Steak

Prep time: 25 minutes | Cook time: 25 minutes | Serves: 6

900g sirloin steaks	2 garlic cloves, thinly sliced
1½ tablespoons tamari sauce	2 tablespoons Irish whiskey
⅓ teaspoon cayenne pepper	2 tablespoons olive oil
⅓ teaspoon ground ginger	Fine sea salt, to taste

1. Add all the ingredients, minus the olive oil and the steak, to a re-sealable plastic bag. 2. Throw in the steak and let it marinate for a couple of hours. After that, drizzle the sirloin steaks with 2 tablespoons olive oil. 3. Insert the crisper plates in the baskets. Divide the steaks between the baskets in zone 1 and zone 2. 4. Select ROAST mode, adjust the cooking temperature to 200°C and set the cooking time to 22 minutes. 5. Press the MATCH COOK button and copy the zone 1 settings to zone 2. 6. Press the START/PAUSE button to begin cooking. 7. Flip the steals halfway through cooking. 8. Serve warm.

Beef Cubes with Aubergine

Prep time: 90 minutes | Cook time: 12 minutes | Serves: 4

675g beef stew meat cubes	1 tablespoon Worcestershire sauce
60g mayonnaise	110g pearl onions
60g sour cream	1 small-sized aubergine, 4.5cm cubes
1 tablespoon yellow mustard	Sea salt and ground black pepper, to taste

1. In a mixing bowl, toss all ingredients until everything is well coated. 2. Cover the bowl and let the food marinate in the refrigerator for 1 hour. 3. Soak wooden skewers in water for 15 minutes. 4. Thread the beef cubes, pearl onions and aubergine onto skewers. 5. Insert the crisper plate in the basket in zone 1, and transfer the skewers to it. 6. Select AIR FRY mode, adjust the cooking temperature to 200°C and set the cooking time to 12 minutes. 7. Press the START/PAUSE button to begin cooking. 8. Flip the skewers halfway through cooking. 9. Serve warm.

Chapter 5 Fish and Seafood

Lemon Cod Fillets

Prep time: 20 minutes | Cook time: 10 minutes | Serves: 2

1½ tablespoons sesame oil

½ heaping teaspoon dried parsley flakes

⅓ teaspoon fresh lemon zest, finely grated

2 medium-sized cod fillets

1 teaspoon sea salt flakes

A pinch of salt and pepper

⅓ teaspoon ground black pepper, or more to savor

½ tablespoon fresh lemon juice

1. Season each cod fillet with sea salt flakes, black pepper and dried parsley flakes. 2. Drizzle them with sesame oil. 3. Insert the crisper plate in the basket in zone 1, and transfer the cod fillets to it. 4. Select AIR FRY mode, adjust the cooking temperature to 190°C and set the cooking time to 10 minutes. 5. Press the START/PAUSE button to begin cooking. 6. Prepare the sauce by mixing the other ingredients. 7. Serve cod fillets on four individual plates garnished with the creamy citrus sauce.

Cauliflower & White Fish Cakes

Prep time: 2 hours 20 minutes | Cook time: 15 minutes | Serves: 4

225g cauliflower florets

½ teaspoon English mustard

2 tablespoons butter, room temperature

½ tablespoon coriander, minced

2 tablespoons sour cream

350g cooked white fish

Salt and freshly cracked black pepper, to savor

1. Boil the cauliflower until tender. 2. Purée the cauliflower in the blender. Transfer them to a mixing dish. 3. Stir in the fish, coriander, salt, and black pepper. 4. Add the sour cream, English mustard, and butter; mix until everything's well incorporated. 5. Shape the mixture into patties. 6. Let the patties stay in the refrigerator for about 2 hours. 7. Insert the crisper plate in the basket in zone 1, and transfer the patties to it. 8. Select AIR FRY mode, adjust the cooking temperature to 200°C and set the cooking time to 13 minutes. 9. Press the START/PAUSE button to begin cooking. 10. Serve the dish with some extra English mustard.

Sea Scallops in Beer

Prep time: 1 hour 10 minutes | Cook time: 7 minutes | Serves: 4

900g sea scallops

120ml beer

4 tablespoons butter

2 sprigs rosemary, only leaves

Sea salt and freshly cracked black pepper, to taste

1. In a ceramic dish, mix the sea scallops with beer; let them marinate for 1 hour. 2. Melt the butter in a frying pan and add the rosemary leaves. Stir them for a few minutes. 3. Transfer the butter mixture to the baskets and apportion the sea scallops between the baskets, and season them with salt and black pepper. 4. Select ROAST mode, adjust the cooking temperature to 205°C and set the cooking time to 6 minutes. 5. Press the MATCH COOK button and copy the zone 1 settings to zone 2. 6. Press the START/PAUSE button to begin cooking. 7. Flip the sea scallops halfway through cooking. 8. Serve warm.

Crusted Flounder Fillets

Prep time: 20 minutes | Cook time: 15 minutes | Serves: 2

2 flounder fillets

1 egg

½ teaspoon Worcestershire sauce

30g coconut flour

25g almond flour

½ teaspoon lemon pepper

½ teaspoon coarse sea salt

¼ teaspoon chili powder

1. Rinse and pat dry the flounder fillets. 2. Whisk the egg and Worcestershire sauce in a shallow bowl. In a separate bowl, mix the coconut flour, almond flour, lemon pepper, salt, and chili powder. 3. Dip the fillets into the egg mixture. Lastly, coat the fish fillets with the coconut flour mixture until they are coated on all sides. 4. Insert the crisper plate in the basket in zone 1, and transfer the fillets to it and spray them with oil. 5. Select AIR FRY mode, adjust the cooking temperature to 200°C and set the cooking time to 12 minutes. 6. Press the START/PAUSE button to begin cooking. 7. Flip the fillets after 7 minutes of cooking time. 8. Serve warm.

Fish Gratin

Prep time: 30 minutes | Cook time: 17 minutes | Serves: 4

- 1 tablespoon avocado oil
- 455g hake fillets
- 1 teaspoon garlic powder
- Sea salt and ground white pepper, to taste
- 2 tablespoons shallots, chopped
- 1 pepper, seeded and chopped
- 120g Cottage cheese
- 120g sour cream
- 1 egg, well whisked
- 1 teaspoon yellow mustard
- 1 tablespoon lime juice
- 50g Swiss cheese, shredded

1. Brush the bottom and sides of a casserole dish with avocado oil. Add the hake fillets to the casserole dish and sprinkle with garlic powder, salt, and pepper. 2. Add the chopped shallots and peppers. 3. In a mixing bowl, thoroughly combine the Cottage cheese, sour cream, egg, mustard, and lime juice. Pour the mixture over fish and spread evenly. 4. Insert the crisper plate in the basket in zone 1, and transfer the hake fillets to it. 5. Select AIR FRY mode, adjust the cooking temperature to 190°C and set the cooking time to 17 minutes. 6. Press the START/PAUSE button to begin cooking. 7. Top the hake fillets with the Swiss cheese after 10 minutes of cooking time. 8. Let the dish rest for 10 minutes before slicing and serving.

Coconut Tilapia

Prep time: 20 minutes | Cook time: 12 minutes | Serves: 2

240ml coconut milk

2 tablespoons lime juice

2 tablespoons Shoyu sauce

Salt and white pepper, to taste

1 teaspoon turmeric powder

½ teaspoon ginger powder

½ Thai Bird's Eye chili, seeded and finely chopped

455g tilapia

2 tablespoons olive oil

1. In a mixing bowl, thoroughly combine the coconut milk with the lime juice, Shoyu sauce, salt, pepper, turmeric, ginger, and chili pepper. Add tilapia and let it marinate for 1 hour. 2. Insert the crisper plate in the basket in zone 1, and transfer the tilapia to it. 3. Select AIR FRY mode, adjust the cooking temperature to 205°C and set the cooking time to 12 minutes. 4. Press the START/PAUSE button to begin cooking. 5. Flip the tilapia halfway through cooking. 6. Serve the fish with some extra lime wedges if desired. Enjoy!

French Sea Bass

Prep time: 15 minutes | Cook time: 10 minutes | Serves: 2

1 tablespoon olive oil

Sauce

120g mayonnaise

1 tablespoon capers, drained and chopped

1 tablespoon gherkins, drained and chopped

2 sea bass fillets

2 tablespoons spring onions, finely chopped

2 tablespoons lemon juice

1. Drizzle olive oil all over the fish fillets and transfer to the crisper plate in the basket. 2. Select AIR FRY mode, adjust the cooking temperature to 200°C and set the cooking time to 10 minutes. 3. Press the START/PAUSE button to begin cooking. 4. Flip the fish fillets halfway through cooking. 5. Make the sauce by whisking the remaining ingredients until everything is well incorporated. Place in the refrigerator until ready to serve.

Sole Fish and Cauliflower Fritters

Prep time: 30 minutes | Cook time: 25 minutes | Serves: 2

225g sole fillets

225g mashed cauliflower

1 egg, well beaten

80g red onion, chopped

2 garlic cloves, minced

2 tablespoons fresh parsley, chopped

1 pepper, finely chopped

½ teaspoon scotch bonnet pepper, minced

1 tablespoon olive oil

1 tablespoon coconut aminos

½ teaspoon paprika

Salt and white pepper, to taste

1. Insert the crisper plate in the basket in zone 1, and transfer the sole fillets to it. 2. Select AIR FRY mode, adjust the cooking temperature to 200°C and set the cooking time to 10 minutes. 3. Press the START/PAUSE button to begin cooking. 4. In a mixing bowl, mash the sole fillets into flakes. Stir in the remaining ingredients. 5. Shape the fish mixture into patties. 6. Transfer the chicken thighs to the crisper plate. 7. Select BAKE mode, adjust the cooking temperature to 200°C and set the cooking time to 14 minutes. 8. Press the START/PAUSE button to begin cooking. 9. Flip the patties halfway through cooking. 10. Serve warm.

Salmon Burgers

Prep time: 15 minutes | Cook time: 10 minutes | Serves: 4

455g salmon

1 egg

1 garlic clove, minced

2 green onions, minced

100g parmesan cheese

Sauce

1 teaspoon rice wine

1½ tablespoons soy sauce

A pinch of salt

1 teaspoon gochugaru (Korean red chili pepper flakes)

1. Mix the salmon, egg, garlic, green onions, and parmesan cheese in a bowl; knead with your hands until everything is well incorporated. 2. Shape the mixture into equally sized patties. 3. Insert the crisper plate in the basket in zone 1, and transfer the patties to it. 4. Select AIR FRY mode, adjust the cooking temperature to 190°C and set the cooking time to 10 minutes. 5. Press the START/PAUSE button to begin cooking. 6. Flip the patties halfway through cooking. 7. Whisk all of the sauce ingredients. 8. Serve the warm fish patties with the sauce on the side.

Crusted Tilapia Fillets

Prep time: 20 minutes | Cook time: 16 minutes | Serves: 5

2 tablespoons ground flaxseeds

1 teaspoon paprika

Sea salt and white pepper, to taste

1 teaspoon garlic paste

2 tablespoons extra-virgin olive oil

60g pecans, ground

5 tilapia fillets, slice into halves

1. Combine the ground flaxseeds, paprika, salt, white pepper, garlic paste, olive oil, and ground pecans in a Ziploc bag. Add the fish fillets and shake to coat well. 2. Insert the crisper plates in the baskets. 3. Divide the fish fillets between the baskets in zone 1 and zone 2. 4. Select AIR FRY mode, adjust the cooking temperature to 205°C and set the cooking time to 16 minutes. 5. Press the MATCH COOK button and copy the zone 1 settings to zone 2. 6. Press the START/PAUSE button to begin cooking. 7. Flip the fillets after 10 minutes of cooking time. 8. You can serve the dish with lemon wedges.

Garlicky Prawns

Prep time: 35 minutes | Cook time: 5 minutes | Serves: 4

18 prawns, shelled and deveined

2 tablespoons freshly squeezed lemon juice

½ teaspoon hot paprika

½ teaspoon salt

1 teaspoon lemon-pepper seasoning

2 tablespoons extra-virgin olive oil

2 garlic cloves, peeled and minced

1 teaspoon onion powder

¼ teaspoon cumin powder

20g fresh parsley, coarsely chopped

1. Place all the ingredients in a mixing dish and gently stir them; cover the dish and let the food marinate for 30 minutes in the refrigerator. 2. Insert the crisper plate in the basket in zone 1, and transfer the prawns to it. 3. Select AIR FRY mode, adjust the cooking temperature to 205°C and set the cooking time to 5 minutes. 4. Press the START/PAUSE button to begin cooking. 5. Serve warm.

Salmon Steaks with Butter and Wine

Prep time: 45 minutes | Cook time: 10 minutes | Serves: 4

2 cloves garlic, minced

4 tablespoons butter, melted

Sea salt and ground black pepper, to taste

1 teaspoon smoked paprika

½ teaspoon onion powder

1 tablespoon lime juice

60ml dry white wine

4 salmon steaks

1. Place all ingredients in a large ceramic dish. Cover the dish and let the food marinate for 30 minutes in the refrigerator. 2. Insert the crisper plates in the baskets. 3. Divide the salmon steaks between the baskets in zone 1 and zone 2. 4. Select BAKE mode, adjust the cooking temperature to 200°C and set the cooking time to 10 minutes. 5. Press the MATCH COOK button and copy the zone 1 settings to zone 2. 6. Press the START/PAUSE button to begin cooking. 7. Flip the salmon steaks and baste them with the reserved marinade halfway through cooking. 8. When done, the salmon steaks should be easily flaked with fork. 9. Serve warm.

Lemony Prawns

Prep time: 10 minutes | Cook time: 10 minutes | Serves: 4

1 teaspoon crushed red pepper flakes, or more to taste

2 cloves garlic, finely minced

Garlic pepper, to savor

1½ tablespoons fresh parsley, roughly chopped

455g prawns, deveined

1½ tablespoons lemon juice

4 tablespoons olive oil

Sea salt flakes, to taste

1. In a bowl, thoroughly combine all the ingredients, coating the prawns on all sides. 2. Insert the crisper plate in the basket in zone 1, and transfer the prawns to it. 3. Select ROAST mode, adjust the cooking temperature to 195°C and set the cooking time to 8 minutes. 4. Press the START/PAUSE button to begin cooking. 5. Serve warm.

Tilapia with Caper Sauce

Prep time: 15 minutes | Cook time: 15 minutes | Serves: 4

4 tilapia fillets

1 tablespoon extra-virgin olive oil

For the Creamy Caper Sauce

120g crème fraîche

2 tablespoons mayonnaise

Celery salt, to taste

Freshly cracked pink peppercorns, to taste

60g Cottage cheese, at room temperature

1 tablespoon capers, finely chopped

1. Toss the tilapia fillets with olive oil, celery salt, and cracked peppercorns until they are well coated. 2. Insert the crisper plates in the baskets. 3. Divide the tilapia fillets between the baskets in zone 1 and zone 2. 4. Select AIR FRY mode, adjust the cooking temperature to 180°C and set the cooking time to 12 minutes. 5. Press the MATCH COOK button and copy the zone 1 settings to zone 2. 6. Press the START/PAUSE button to begin cooking. 7. Flip the tilapia fillets halfway through cooking. 8. Whisk all of the sauce ingredients. 9. Garnish air-fried tilapia fillets with the sauce and serve immediately!

Flounder with Chives

Prep time: 15 minutes | Cook time: 12 minutes | Serves: 4

4 flounder fillets

Sea salt and freshly cracked mixed peppercorns, to taste

1½ tablespoons dark sesame oil

2 tablespoons sake

60ml soy sauce

1 tablespoon grated lemon rind

2 garlic cloves, minced

2 tablespoons chopped chives, to serve

1. Place all the ingredients, without the chives, in a large-sized mixing dish. Cover the dish and allow the fillets to marinate for about 2 hours in the fridge. 2. Insert the crisper plates in the baskets. 3. Divide the fillets between the baskets in zone 1 and zone 2. 4. Select AIR FRY mode, adjust the cooking temperature to 180°C and set the cooking time to 12 minutes. 5. Press the MATCH COOK button and copy the zone 1 settings to zone 2. 6. Press the START/PAUSE button to begin cooking. 7. Flip the fillets halfway through cooking. 8. Pour the remaining marinade into a pan that is preheated over a medium-low heat; let it simmer, stirring continuously, until it has thickened. 9. Pour the prepared glaze over flounder and serve garnished with fresh chives.

Crab & Cauliflower Cakes

Prep time: 20 minutes | Cook time: 12 minutes | Serves: 4

1½ tablespoons mayonnaise

½ teaspoon whole-grain mustard

2 eggs, well beaten

⅓ teaspoon ground black pepper

225g smashed cauliflower

½ teaspoon dried dill weed

225g crabmeat

A pinch of salt

1½ tablespoons softened butter

1. Mix all the ingredients thoroughly. Shape the mixture into 4 patties. 2. Insert the crisper plate in the basket in zone 1, and transfer the chicken thighs to it. 3. Select AIR FRY mode, adjust the cooking temperature to 185°C and set the cooking time to 12 minutes. 4. Press the START/PAUSE button to begin cooking. 5. Flip the patties halfway through cooking. 6. Serve the patties over boiled potatoes.

Salmon with Coriander Sauce

Prep time: 50 minutes | Cook time: 10 minutes | Serves: 4

675g salmon steak

½ teaspoon grated lemon zest

Freshly cracked mixed peppercorns, to taste

80ml lemon juice

Fresh chopped chives, for garnish

120ml dry white wine

½ teaspoon fresh coriander, chopped

Fine sea salt, to taste

1. Place all ingredients, except for salmon steak and chives, in a deep pan. Bring to a boil over medium-high flame until it has reduced by half. Allow it to cool down. 2. Allow the salmon steak to marinate in the refrigerator for about 40 minutes. 3. Insert the crisper plate in the basket in zone 1, and transfer the salmon steak to it. 4. Select AIR FRY mode, adjust the cooking temperature to 205°C and set the cooking time to 10 minutes. 5. Press the START/PAUSE button to begin cooking. 6. Brush the salmon steak with the reserved marinade and garnish with fresh chopped chives.

Rockfish Fillets with Avocado Cream

Prep time: 15 minutes | Cook time: 10 minutes | Serves: 4

For the Fish Fillets

1½ tablespoons balsamic vinegar

120ml vegetable stock

⅓ teaspoon shallot powder

1 tablespoon soy sauce

4 Rockfish fillets

1 teaspoon ground black pepper

1½ tablespoons olive oil

Fine sea salt, to taste

⅓ teaspoon garlic powder

For the Avocado Cream:

2 tablespoons Greek-style yogurt

1 clove garlic, peeled and minced

1 teaspoon ground black pepper

½ tablespoon olive oil

80ml vegetable stock

1 avocado

½ teaspoon lime juice

⅓ teaspoon fine sea salt

1. In a bowl, wash and pat the fillets dry using some paper towels. Add all the seasonings. 2. In another bowl, stir in the remaining ingredients for the fish fillets. 3. Add the seasoned fish fillets; cover the bowl and let the fillets marinate in your refrigerator at least 3 hours. 4. Insert the crisper plates in the baskets. Divide the fillets between the baskets in zone 1 and zone 2. 5. Select AIR FRY mode, adjust the cooking temperature to 160°C and set the cooking time to 9 minutes. 6. Press the MATCH COOK button and copy the zone 1 settings to zone 2. 7. Press the START/PAUSE button to begin cooking. 8. Mix all of the cream ingredients in a blender. 9. Serve the rockfish fillets topped with the avocado cream.

Cod Fillets with Lemon

Prep time: 20 minutes | Cook time: 10 minutes | Serves: 2

2 medium-sized cod fillets

½ tablespoon fresh lemon juice

1½ tablespoons olive oil

½ tablespoon whole-grain mustard

Sea salt and ground black pepper, to savor

60g coconut flour

2 eggs

1. Thoroughly combine olive oil and coconut flour in a shallow bowl. 2. In another shallow bowl, whisk the egg. 3. Drizzle each cod fillet with lemon juice and spread with mustard. Sprinkle each fillet with salt and ground black pepper. 4. Dip each fish fillet into the whisked egg; now, roll each of them in the olive oil/breadcrumb mix. 5. Insert the crisper plates in the baskets. Divide the cod fillets between the baskets in zone 1 and zone 2. 6. Select AIR FRY mode, adjust the cooking temperature to 180°C and set the cooking time to 10 minutes. 7. Press the MATCH COOK button and copy the zone 1 settings to zone 2. 8. Press the START/PAUSE button to begin cooking. 9. Flip the cod fillets halfway through cooking. 10. Serve the dish with potato salad.

Crab Cakes with Capers

Prep time: 20 minutes | Cook time: 12 minutes | Serves: 5

⅓ teaspoon ground black pepper

½ tablespoon nonpareil capers

3 eggs, well whisked

½ teaspoon dried dill weed

1½ tablespoons softened butter

½ teaspoon whole-grain mustard

225g crabmeat

100g Romano cheese, grated

2 ½ tablespoons mayonnaise

A pinch of salt

1. Mix all the ingredients thoroughly. 2. Shape the mixture into 4 balls and press each ball to form the cakes. 3. Spritz your cakes with cooking oil. 4. Insert the crisper plates in the baskets. Divide the cakes between the baskets in zone 1 and zone 2. 5. Select BAKE mode, adjust the cooking temperature to 185°C and set the cooking time to 12 minutes. 6. Press the MATCH COOK button and copy the zone 1 settings to zone 2. 7. Press the START/PAUSE button to begin cooking. 8. Flip the cakes halfway through cooking. 9. Serve warm.

Chapter 6 Snacks and Starters

Banana Peppers with Cheese

Prep time: 10 minutes | Cook time: 20 minutes | Serves: 4

200g banana peppers, chopped

1 tablespoon avocado oil

1 tablespoon dried oregano

2 tablespoons mascarpone

100g Monterey Jack cheese, shredded

1. Brush a suitable baking pan with avocado oil. 2. Mix banana peppers with dried oregano and mascarpone and put in the prepared baking pan. 3. Top the peppers with Monterey Jack cheese. 4. Transfer the pan to the basket in zone 1. 5. Select BAKE mode, adjust the cooking temperature to 185°C and set the cooking time to 20 minutes. 6. Press the START/PAUSE button to begin cooking.

Parmesan Cauliflower

Prep time: 10 minutes | Cook time: 20 minutes | Serves: 2

180g cauliflower, chopped

25g Parmesan, grated

1 tablespoon avocado oil

1. Sprinkle the cauliflower with avocado oil. 2. Insert the crisper plate in the basket in zone 1, and transfer the food to it. 3. Select AIR FRY mode, adjust the cooking temperature to 200°C and set the cooking time to 20 minutes. 4. Press the START/PAUSE button to begin cooking. 5. Toss the food and sprinkle them with Parmesan halfway through cooking. 6. Serve warm.

Keto Coleslaw

Prep time: 10 minutes | Cook time: 20 minutes | Serves: 4

90g white cabbage, shredded

2 tablespoons apple cider vinegar

120g heavy cream

1 teaspoon ground black pepper

1 tablespoon Dijon mustard

1. Mix white cabbage with heavy cream. 2. Transfer the food to the basket in zone 1. 3. Select ROAST mode, adjust the cooking temperature to 175°C and set the cooking time to 20 minutes. 4. Press the START/PAUSE button to begin cooking. 5. Stir the food from time to time. 6. Transfer the white cabbage mixture in the salad bowl. 7. Add all remaining ingredients and carefully mix.

Coconut Brussels Sprouts

Prep time: 10 minutes | Cook time: 15 minutes | Serves: 4

200g Brussels sprouts

1 tablespoon coconut shred

1 tablespoon coconut oil

1 teaspoon ground paprika

1 teaspoon ground black pepper

1. Toss all ingredients in the basket in zone 1. 2. ROAST the food at 190°C for 15 minutes. 3. Stir the food every 5 minutes. 4. Serve warm.

Mustard Cabbage Steaks

Prep time: 10 minutes | Cook time: 25 minutes | Serves: 4

455g white cabbage, cut into steaks
1 tablespoon avocado oil
1 teaspoon salt
1 teaspoon apple cider vinegar
½ teaspoon mustard

1. Rub the white cabbage steaks with avocado oil, salt, apple cider vinegar, and mustard. 2. Insert the crisper plate in the basket in zone 1, and transfer the food to it. 3. Select AIR FRY mode, adjust the cooking temperature to 190°C and set the cooking time to 25 minutes. 4. Press the START/PAUSE button to begin cooking. 5. Flip the food after 15 minutes of cooking time.

Cheese Tomatillos Slices

Prep time: 10 minutes | Cook time: 5 minutes | Serves: 4

2 tomatillos
25g almond flour
2 eggs, beaten
¼ teaspoon ground black pepper
¼ teaspoon chili powder
25g Monterey Jack cheese, shredded
4 lettuce leaves

1. Slice the tomatillos into 4 slices and sprinkle with ground black pepper and chili powder. 2. Dip the tomatillos in the eggs and coat in the almond flour. Repeat this step one more time. 3. Insert the crisper plate in the basket in zone 1, and transfer the food to it. 4. Select AIR FRY mode, adjust the cooking temperature to 205°C and set the cooking time to 4 minutes. 5. Press the START/PAUSE button to begin cooking. 6. Flip the food halfway through cooking. 7. Put the cooked tomatillos on the lettuce leaves and top with Monterey Jack cheese.

Turnip Bites

Prep time: 10 minutes | Cook time: 20 minutes | Serves: 4

125g turnip, cut into fries

4 tablespoons avocado oil

1 teaspoon garlic powder

1. Mix turnip with garlic powder and avocado oil and transfer them to the crisper plate in the basket. 2. AIR FRY the turnip bites at 180°C for 20 minutes. 3. Toss them from time to time to avoid burning.

Cream Cauliflower

Prep time: 10 minutes | Cook time: 10 minutes | Serves: 4

180g cauliflower, chopped

1 teaspoon avocado oil

1 teaspoon salt

1 teaspoon dried oregano

50g Monterey Jack, shredded

120g of heavy cream

½ teaspoon coconut oil

1. Put the cauliflower in the basket. 2. Sprinkle them with avocado oil, salt, dried oregano, heavy cream, and coconut oil. 3. Toss them and top them with the Monterey Jack cheese. 4. BAKE the dish at 205°C for 10 minutes.

Cheese Asparagus

Prep time: 10 minutes | Cook time: 5 minutes | Serves: 3

225g Asparagus

25g Parmesan, grated

1 teaspoon avocado oil

1. Chop the asparagus roughly and sprinkle with avocado oil. 2. Insert the crisper plate in the basket in zone 1, and transfer the food to it. 3. Select AIR FRY mode, adjust the cooking temperature to 205°C and set the cooking time to 5 minutes. 4. Press the START/PAUSE button to begin cooking. 5. Transfer the cooked asparagus in the serving plate and sprinkle with Parmesan.

Cauliflower and Asparagus

Prep time: 5 minutes | Cook time: 20 minutes | Serves: 4

90g cauliflower, chopped

150g asparagus, chopped

1 tablespoon coconut oil

1 teaspoon Italian seasonings

1 teaspoon salt

1. Mix all of the ingredients in the basket in zone 1. 2. ROAST the food at 190°C for 20 minutes, tossing them halfway through cooking. 3. Serve warm.

Yummy Chicken Bites

Prep time: 10 minutes | Cook time: 20 minutes | Serves: 4

1 teaspoon onion powder

455g chicken breast, skinless, boneless, chopped

1 teaspoon chili powder

1 teaspoon coconut oil

1. Mix chicken breast with onion powder, chili powder, and coconut oil. 2. Insert the crisper plate in the basket in zone 1, and transfer the meat to it. 3. Select AIR FRY mode, adjust the cooking temperature to 190°C and set the cooking time to 20 minutes. 4. Press the START/PAUSE button to begin cooking. 5. Flip the meat halfway through cooking.

Courgette Slices with Mozzarella Cheese

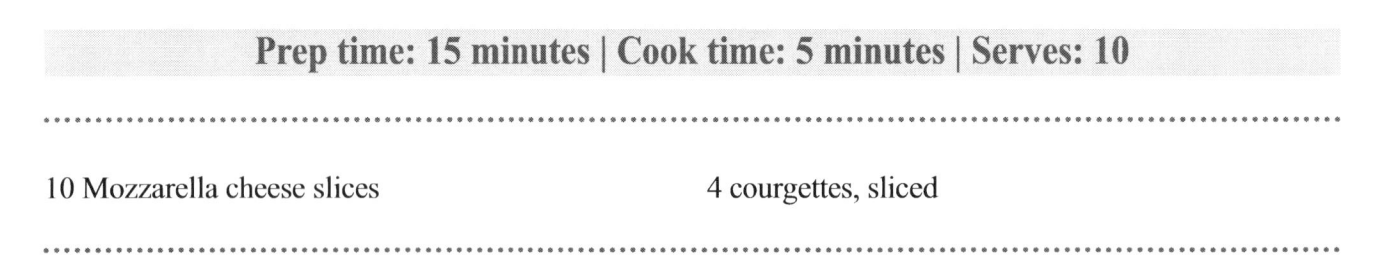

Prep time: 15 minutes | Cook time: 5 minutes | Serves: 10

10 Mozzarella cheese slices

4 courgettes, sliced

1. Put the Mozzarella slices on the courgette slices and fold them. 2. Secure the turnovers with a toothpick if needed. 3. Insert the crisper plates in the baskets. Divide the food between the baskets in zone 1 and zone 2. 4. Select AIR FRY mode, adjust the cooking temperature to 205°C and set the cooking time to 3 minutes. 5. Press the MATCH COOK button and copy the zone 1 settings to zone 2. 6. Press the START/PAUSE button to begin cooking. 7. Serve hot.

Cheese Kale Chips

Prep time: 5 minutes | Cook time: 30 minutes | Serves: 8

50g Parmesan, grated

300g kale, roughly chopped

1. Mix kale with Parmesan and transfer them to the baskets in the zones. 2. ROAST the food at 175°C for 30 minutes, tossing them after 10 minutes. 3. Serve warm.

Mozzarella Portobello Pizza

Prep time: 10 minutes | Cook time: 7 minutes | Serves: 6

6 Portobello mushroom caps

1 tomato, chopped

120g Mozzarella, shredded

1 teaspoon dried basil

1 teaspoon coconut oil

1. Insert the crisper plate in the basket in zone 1, and transfer the Portobello mushroom cups to it; top them with tomato, dried basil, and Mozzarella. 2. Select AIR FRY mode, adjust the cooking temperature to 205°C and set the cooking time to 7 minutes. 3. Press the START/PAUSE button to begin cooking. 4. Serve warm.

Easy Parmesan Chips

Prep time: 5 minutes | Cook time: 5 minutes | Serves: 4

150g Parmesan, grated

1. Make the small circles from the grated cheese. 2. Insert the crisper plate in the basket in zone 1, and transfer the food to it. 3. Select AIR FRY mode, adjust the cooking temperature to 205°C and set the cooking time to 5 minutes. 4. Press the START/PAUSE button to begin cooking. 5. Cool the Parmesan chips before serving.

Courgette Crackers

Prep time: 15 minutes | Cook time: 12 minutes | Serves: 8

130g courgette, grated
2 tablespoons flax meal
2 tablespoons coconut flour
1 teaspoon coconut oil
1 egg, beaten

1. Mix courgette with flax meal, coconut flour, and egg. 2. Roll the dough and make the crackers. 3. Transfer the food to the basket in zone 1. 4. Select BAKE mode, adjust the cooking temperature to 205°C and set the cooking time to 12 minutes. 5. Press the START/PAUSE button to begin cooking. 6. Flip the food halfway through cooking. 7. Serve the golden brown courgette.

Olives Cakes

Prep time: 10 minutes | Cook time: 12 minutes | Serves: 6

2 tablespoons fresh coriander, chopped

1 egg, beaten

60g coconut flour

25g spring onions, chopped

150g kalamata olives, pitted and minced

1. Mix fresh coriander with egg, coconut flour, spring onions, and olives. 2. Make the small cakes and put them in the air fryer on one layer. 3. Cook the cakes at 195°C for 6 minutes per side.

Cheddar Pork Minis

Prep time: 10 minutes | Cook time: 15 minutes | Serves: 4

140g pork mince

1 teaspoon Italian seasonings

25g Cheddar cheese, shredded

1 teaspoon tomato paste

½ teaspoon coconut oil

1. In the mixing bowl, mix pork mince with Italian seasonings, Cheddar cheese, and tomato paste. 2. Make the minis from the mixture. 3. Insert the crisper plate in the basket in zone 1, and transfer the minis to it. 4. Select AIR FRY mode, adjust the cooking temperature to 190°C and set the cooking time to 15 minutes. 5. Press the START/PAUSE button to begin cooking. 6. Serve hot.

Chapter 7 Desserts

Chocolate Raspberry Cake

Prep time: 30 minutes | Cook time: 30 minutes | Serves: 4

65g monk fruit

55g unsalted butter, room temperature

1 egg plus 1 egg white, lightly whisked

75g almond flour

For the Filling

50g fresh raspberries

65g monk fruit

2 tablespoons Dutch-process cocoa powder

½ teaspoon ground cinnamon

1 tablespoon candied ginger

⅛ teaspoon table salt

1 teaspoon fresh lime juice

1. Spritz the inside of two cake pans with the butter-flavoured cooking spray. 2. In a mixing bowl, beat the monk fruit and butter until creamy and uniform. Then, stir in the whisked eggs. Stir in the almond flour, cocoa powder, cinnamon, ginger and salt. 3. Press the batter into the cake pans; use a wide spatula to level the surface of the batter. 4. Transfer the pan to the basket in zone 1. 5. Select BAKE mode, adjust the cooking temperature to 160°C and set the cooking time to 20 minutes. 6. Press the START/PAUSE button to begin cooking. 7. While the cake is baking, stir together all of the ingredients for the filling in a medium saucepan. 8. Cook them over high heat, stirring frequently and mashing with the back of a spoon; bring to a boil and decrease the temperature. 9. Continue to cook, stirring until the mixture thickens, for another 7 minutes. Let the filling cool to room temperature. 10. Spread ½ of raspberry filling over the first crust. Top with another crust; spread remaining filling over top. 11. Spread frosting over top and sides of your cake. Enjoy!

White Chocolate Cookies

Prep time: 40 minutes | Cook time: 11 minutes | Serves: 10

185g butter

165g almond flour

60g coconut flour

2 tablespoons coconut oil

20g granulated sweetener

⅓ teaspoon ground anise star

⅓ teaspoon ground allspice

⅓ teaspoon grated nutmeg

¼ teaspoon fine sea salt

200g white chocolate, unsweetened

2 eggs, well beaten

1. Put all of the above ingredients, minus 1 egg, into a mixing dish, and knead them with your hand until soft dough is formed. 2. Let the dough stay in the refrigerator for 20 minutes. 3. Roll the chilled dough into small balls; flatten the balls. 4. Make an egg wash by using the remaining egg. Then, glaze the cookies with the egg wash. 5. Insert the crisper plates in the baskets. Divide the cookies between the baskets in zone 1 and zone 2. 6. Select BAKE mode, adjust the cooking temperature to 175°C and set the cooking time to 11 minutes. 7. Press the MATCH COOK button and copy the zone 1 settings to zone 2. 8. Press the START/PAUSE button to begin cooking. 9. Serve warm.

Puffy Pecan Cookies

Prep time: 30 minutes | Cook time: 15 minutes | Serves: 10

- 180ml coconut oil, room temperature
- 180g coconut flour
- 120g pecan nuts, unsalted and roughly chopped
- 3 eggs plus an egg yolk, whisked
- 150g extra-fine almond flour
- 150g monk fruit
- ¼ teaspoon freshly grated nutmeg
- ⅓ teaspoon ground cloves
- ½ teaspoon baking powder
- ⅓ teaspoon baking soda
- ½ teaspoon pure vanilla extract
- ½ teaspoon pure coconut extract
- ⅛ teaspoon fine sea salt

1. In a bowl, combine both types of flour, baking soda and baking powder. 2. In a separate bowl, beat the eggs with coconut oil. Combine egg mixture with the flour mixture. 3. Throw in the other ingredients, mixing well. Shape the mixture into cookies. 4. Insert the crisper plates in the baskets. Divide the cookies between the baskets in zone 1 and zone 2. 5. Select BAKE mode, adjust the cooking temperature to 190°C and set the cooking time to 25 minutes. 6. Press the MATCH COOK button and copy the zone 1 settings to zone 2. 7. Press the START/PAUSE button to begin cooking. 8. Serve warm.

Flourless Almond Cookies

Prep time: 50 minutes | Cook time: 15 minutes | Serves: 8

60g slivered almonds

115g butter, room temperature

100g monk fruit

65g blanched almond flour

40g coconut flour

⅓ teaspoon ground cloves

1 tablespoon ginger powder

¾ teaspoon pure vanilla extract

1. In a mixing dish, beat the monk fruit, butter, vanilla extract, ground cloves, and ginger until light and fluffy. Then, throw in the coconut flour, almond flour, and slivered almonds. 2. Continue mixing until it forms a soft dough. Cover the dish and place in the refrigerator to chill them for 35 minutes. 3. Roll dough into small cookies and gently press them. 4. Insert the crisper plates in the baskets. Divide the food between the baskets in zone 1 and zone 2. 5. Select BAKE mode, adjust the cooking temperature to 160°C and set the cooking time to 13 minutes. 6. Press the MATCH COOK button and copy the zone 1 settings to zone 2. 7. Press the START/PAUSE button to begin cooking. 8. Serve and enjoy.

Walnuts Tart

Prep time: 20 minutes | Cook time: 15 minutes | Serves: 6

240ml coconut milk

2 eggs

55g butter, at room temperature

1 teaspoon vanilla essence

¼ teaspoon ground cardamom

¼ teaspoon ground cloves

60g walnuts, ground

15g sweetener

60g almond flour

1. Spritz the sides and bottom of a baking pan with nonstick cooking spray. 2. Mix all ingredients until well combined. 3. Scrape the batter into the prepared baking pan. 4. Transfer the pan to the basket in zone 1. 5. Select BAKE mode, adjust the cooking temperature to 180°C and set the cooking time to 13 minutes. 6. Press the START/PAUSE button to begin cooking. 7. Serve warm.

Old-Fashioned Raspberries Muffins

Prep time: 20 minutes | Cook time: 15 minutes | Serves: 6

65g raspberries

20g sweetener

60g coconut oil

240g sour cream

1¼ teaspoons baking powder

200g almond flour

2 eggs

⅓ teaspoon ground allspice

⅓ teaspoon ground anise star

½ teaspoon grated lemon zest

¼ teaspoon salt

1. In the first bowl, thoroughly combine the almond flour, baking powder, sweetener, salt, anise, and allspice and lemon zest. 2. In the second bowl, whisk coconut oil, sour cream, and eggs; whisk to combine well. Add the wet mixture to the dry mixture. Fold in the raspberries. 3. Press the batter mixture into a lightly greased muffin tin. 4. Transfer the muffin tin to the basket in zone 1. 5. Select BAKE mode, adjust the cooking temperature to 175°C and set the cooking time to 15 minutes. 6. Press the START/PAUSE button to begin cooking. 7. Use a toothpick to check. 8. Serve warm.

Double Chocolate Brownies

Prep time: 55 minutes | Cook time: 20 minutes | Serves: 10

3 tablespoons whiskey

200g white chocolate

75g almond flour

25g coconut flakes

120ml coconut oil

2 eggs plus an egg yolk, whisked

150g monk fruit

2 tablespoons cocoa powder, unsweetened

¼ teaspoon ground cardamom

1 teaspoon pure rum extract

1. Microwave white chocolate and coconut oil until everything's melted; allow the mixture to cool at room temperature. 2. Thoroughly whisk the eggs, monk fruit, rum extract, cocoa powder and cardamom. 3. Add the rum mixture to the chocolate mixture. Stir in the flour and coconut flakes; mix them to combine. 4. Mix cranberries with whiskey and let them soak for 15 minutes. Fold them into the batter. Press the batter into a lightly buttered cake pan. 5. Transfer the pan to the basket in zone 1. 6. Select BAKE mode, adjust the cooking temperature to 170°C and set the cooking time to 35 minutes. 7. Allow them to cool slightly on a wire rack before slicing and serving.

Blackberry Muffins

Prep time: 20 minutes | Cook time: 15 minutes | Serves: 8

150g almond flour

½ teaspoon baking soda

1 teaspoon baking powder

¼ teaspoon salt

15g sweetener

2 eggs, whisked

120ml milk

60ml coconut oil, melted

½ teaspoon vanilla paste

75g fresh blackberries

1. In a mixing bowl, combine the almond flour, baking soda, baking powder, sweetener, and salt. Whisk to combine well. 2. In another mixing bowl, mix the eggs, milk, coconut oil, and vanilla. 3. Add the wet egg mixture to dry the flour mixture. Then, carefully fold in the fresh blackberries; gently stir to combine. 4. Scrape the batter mixture into the muffin cups. 5. Insert the crisper plates in the baskets. Divide the muffin cups between the baskets in zone 1 and zone 2. 6. Select BAKE mode, adjust the cooking temperature to 175°C and set the cooking time to 12 minutes. 7. Press the MATCH COOK button and copy the zone 1 settings to zone 2. 8. Press the START/PAUSE button to begin cooking. Flip the food halfway through cooking. 9. Sprinkle some extra icing sugar over the top of each muffin if desired. Serve and enjoy!

Cookies with Chocolate Chips

Prep time: 20 minutes | Cook time: 15 minutes | Serves: 8

- 115g butter, at room temperature
- 40g sweetener
- 65g chunky peanut butter
- 1 teaspoon vanilla paste
- 100g almond flour
- 80g coconut flour
- 35g cocoa powder, unsweetened
- 1½ teaspoons baking powder
- ¼ teaspoon ground cinnamon
- ¼ teaspoon crystallized ginger
- 85g chocolate chips, unsweetened

1. In a mixing dish, beat the butter and sweetener until creamy and uniform. Stir in the peanut butter and vanilla. 2. In another mixing dish, thoroughly combine the flour, cocoa powder, baking powder, cinnamon, and crystallized ginger. 3. Add the flour mixture to the peanut butter mixture; mix to combine well. Afterwards, fold in the chocolate chips. 4. Insert the crisper plates in the baskets and line them with parchment paper. 5. Divide the food between the baskets in zone 1 and zone 2. 6. Select BAKE mode, adjust the cooking temperature to 185°C and set the cooking time to 11 minutes. 7. Press the MATCH COOK button and copy the zone 1 settings to zone 2. 8. Press the START/PAUSE button to begin cooking. 9. Bon appétit!

Keto Berry Crumble Pots

Prep time: 40 minutes | Cook time: 35 minutes | Serves: 6

50g unsweetened mixed berries

15g granulated sweetener

2 tablespoons golden flaxseed meal

¼ teaspoon ground star anise

½ teaspoon ground cinnamon

1 teaspoon xanthan gum

65g almond flour

30g powdered sweetener

½ teaspoon baking powder

35g unsweetened coconut, finely shredded

55g butter, cut into small pieces

1. Toss the mixed berries with the granulated sweetener, golden flaxseed meal, star anise, cinnamon, and xanthan gum. Divide between six custard cups coated with cooking spray. 2. In a mixing dish, thoroughly combine the remaining ingredients. Sprinkle over the berry mixture. 3. BAKE the food in both zones at 165°C for 35 minutes. 4. Serve warm.

Vanilla Chocolate Cake

Prep time: 40 minutes | Cook time: 30 minutes | Serves: 8

150g almond flour

50g coconut meal

20g sweetener

1 teaspoon baking powder

¼ teaspoon salt

115g butter, melted

120ml hot strongly brewed coffee

½ teaspoon vanilla

1 egg

Topping

30g coconut flour

20g powdered sweetener

½ teaspoon ground cardamom

1 teaspoon ground cinnamon

3 tablespoons coconut oil

1. Mix all dry ingredients for your cake; then, mix in the wet ingredients. Mix them until everything is well incorporated. 2. Spritz a suitable baking pan with cooking spray. Scrape the batter into the baking pan. 3. Make the topping by mixing all ingredients. Place them on top of the cake. Smooth the top with a spatula. 4. Transfer the pan to the basket in zone 1. 5. Select BAKE mode, adjust the cooking temperature to 165°C and set the cooking time to 30 minutes. 6. Press the START/PAUSE button to begin cooking. 7. The top of the cake should spring back when gently pressed with your fingers. 8. Serve the dish with your favorite hot beverage.

Chocolate Fudge Cake

Prep time: 30 minutes | Cook time: 22 minutes | Serves: 10

250g peanut butter

225g monk fruit

3 eggs

100g almond flour

1 teaspoon baking powder

¼ teaspoon salt

140g cooking chocolate, broken into chunks

1. Spritz the sides and bottom of a suitable baking pan with cooking spray. 2. Thoroughly combine the peanut butter with the monk fruit in the pan until creamy. Fold in the egg and beat until fluffy. 3. Stir in the almond flour, baking powder, salt, and bakers' chocolate. Mix them until everything is well combined. 4. Transfer the pan to the basket in zone 1. 5. Select BAKE mode, adjust the cooking temperature to 175°C and set the cooking time to 22 minutes. 6. Press the START/PAUSE button to begin cooking. 7. Transfer the pan to a wire rack to cool the dish before slicing and serving.

Puffy Coconut Cookies

Prep time: 20 minutes | Cook time: 10 minutes | Serves: 12

230g butter, melted

50g granulated sweetener

3 eggs

2 tablespoons coconut milk

1 teaspoon coconut extract

1 teaspoon vanilla extract

120g coconut flour

125g almond flour

½ teaspoon baking powder

½ teaspoon baking soda

½ teaspoon fine table salt

50g coconut chips, unsweetened

1. In the bowl of an electric mixer, beat the butter and sweetener until well combined. Now, add the eggs one at a time, and mix well; add the coconut milk, coconut extract, and vanilla; beat until creamy and uniform. 2. Mix the flour with baking powder, baking soda, and salt. Then, stir the flour mixture into the butter mixture and stir until everything is well incorporated. 3. Fold in the coconut chips and mix again. Scoop out 1 tablespoon size balls of the batter on a cookie pan, leaving 5 cm between each cookie. 4. BAKE the food in both zones at 175°C for 10 minutes, flipping them once or twice during cooking. 5. Let the cookies cool on wire racks.

Conclusion

If you're looking for an air fryer that can do it all, the Ninja Foodi 2-Basket Air Fryer is a great option. It features two baskets that can be used independently or together, allowing you to cook multiple items at the same time. The air fryer also has a dehydrator function, so you can make your healthy snacks like dehydrated fruit or veggie chips. Plus, it comes with a handy recipe book to get you started. The Ninja Foodi 2-Basket Air Fryer is a versatile appliance that can help you coop a variety of healthy and delicious meals. If you're looking for an air fryer that can do it all, the Ninja Foodi 2-Basket Air Fryer is a great option.

Appendix Recipes Index

A

Aromatic Turkey Breast 39
Asian Steak Strips 55

B

Bacon-Wrapped Turkey 38
Banana Peppers with Cheese 77
Beef Bulgogi Burgers 54
Beef Chops with Coriander 50
Beef Chops with Salad 51
Beef Cubes with Aubergine 61
Beef Tenderloins in Beef Stock 58
Beef with Pearl Onions and Cauliflower 52
Beer-Braised Beef 54
Blackberry Muffins 92
Broccoli Fritters 17

C

Cauliflower & White Fish Cakes 63
Cauliflower and Asparagus 81
Cauliflower and Broccoli 22
Celery & Bacon Croquettes 19
Cheddar Pork Minis 85
Cheese Asparagus 81
Cheese Asparagus Casserole 21
Cheese Cauliflower Balls 13
Cheese Kale Chips 83
Cheese Mushroom Balls 18
Cheese Tomatillos Slices 79
Chicken Sausage Frittata 20
Chicken Sliders in Chili Sauce 44
Chicken with Leeks 44
Chicken with Smoked Bacon 42
Chili Cauliflower Florets 22
Chocolate Fudge Cake 96
Chocolate Raspberry Cake 86
Coated Jicama Sticks 23
Coconut Brussels Sprouts 78
Coconut Chicken Breast 34
Coconut Tilapia 66
Cod Fillets with Lemon 75
Cookies with Chocolate Chips 93
Corn Croquettes 31
Courgette Crackers 84
Courgette Noodles 23
Courgette Slices with Mozzarella Cheese 82
Crab & Cauliflower Cakes 73
Crab Cakes with Capers 76
Cream Cauliflower 80
Creole Gold Potato Wedges 32
Crispy Asparagus Fries 27
Crispy Cheese Spinach Balls 14
Crusted Flounder Fillets 64
Crusted Tilapia Fillets 69

D

Double Chocolate Brownies 91

E

Easy Aubergine Slices 24
Easy Parmesan Chips 84
Easy-to-Make Duck Skin 33
Eggs & Sausage Keto Rolls 37
Eggs with Beef and Tomato 17

F

Filet Mignon Steaks 60
Filet Mignon with Peanut Sauce 56
Fish Gratin 65
Flounder with Chives 72
Flourless Almond Cookies 89
French Sea Bass 66
Fresh Corn on the Cob 31

G

Garlicky Courgette Slices 25
Garlicky Prawns 69
Greek Feta Frittata 14
Greek Omelet with Cheese 15
Green Beans with Ground Coriander 27

I

Italian-Style Chicken Breasts 45

K

Kale in Beef Stock 26
Keto Berry Crumble Pots 94
Keto Coleslaw 78

L

Lemon Cod Fillets 62
Lemon Pepper-Seasoned Cauliflower 29
Lemony Beef Steaks 49
Lemony Prawns 70
Loaded Turkey Meatloaf 41

M

Manchego & Cauliflower Patties 16
Meatballs with Spicy Sauce 59
Mozzarella Portobello Pizza 83
Mustard Cabbage Steaks 79
Mustard Marinated Chicken 34

N

Nutty Turkey Breast 36

O

Old-Fashioned Raspberries Muffins 90
Olives Cakes 85

P

Panko Broccoli Tots 28
Parmesan Cauliflower 77
Pepper Chicken Cutlets 39
Potato Pot with Sauce 30
Puffy Coconut Cookies 97
Puffy Pecan Cookies 88

R

Rich Meatloaf 57
Rockfish Fillets with Avocado Cream 74
Rustic Turkey Breasts 46

S

Salmon Burgers 68
Salmon Steaks with Butter and Wine 70
Salmon with Coriander Sauce 73
Sausage Omelet 16
Sea Scallops in Beer 64
Simple Brussels Sprouts 29
Skinless Chicken Thighs 35
Smoked Tofu Omelet 19
Sole Fish and Cauliflower Fritters 67
Spiced Broccoli Steaks 24
Spicy Steak 58
Spicy Steak Pieces 55
Stuffed Mushrooms 12
Sweet-Sour Chicken Drumsticks 35

T

Tangy Beef Strips 48
Tangy Chicken with Parsley 41
Tarragon-Seasoned Chicken Thighs 36
Tasty Gruyère Stuffed Mushrooms 20
T-Bone Steak with Aromatics 47
Teriyaki Steak 53
Thanksgiving Turkey 40
Tilapia with Caper Sauce 71
Trimmed Asparagus 26
Turkey Thighs with Vegetables 43
Turkey with Cheese and Pasilla Peppers 15
Turmeric Cauliflower Steaks 25
Turnip Bites 80
Typical Chicken Nuggets 38

U

Unseasoned Beetroot 28

V

Vanilla Chocolate Cake 95
Vinegar-Seasoned Chicken Wings 33

W

Walnuts Tart 89
Whisky Steak 61
White Chocolate Cookies 87

Y

Yummy Chicken Bites 82

Printed in Great Britain
by Amazon